Learning to lead

LEARNING TO LEAD

Biblical leadership then and now

Chua Wee Hian

Inter-Varsity Press

Inter-Varsity Press
38 De Montfort Street, Leicester LE1 7GP, England

Unless otherwise stated, quotations from the Bible are taken from the HOLY BIBLE: NEW INTERNATIONAL VERSION, © 1973, 1978, 1984 by the International Bible Society, New York. Published in Great Britain by Hodder and Stoughton.

First published 1987
Reprinted 1988

British Library Cataloguing in Publication Data

Chua, Wee Hian
    Learning to lead: Biblical leadership then
    and now.
    1. Christian leadership
    I. Title
    248.4   BV652.1
    ISBN 0–85110–772–9

Set in Times New Roman

Phototypeset in Great Britain by Input Typesetting Ltd, London SW18 8DR

Printed in Great Britain by Richard Clay Ltd, Bungay, Suffolk

Inter-Varsity Press is the publishing division of the Universities and Colleges Christian Fellowship (formerly the Inter-Varsity Fellowship), a student movement linking Christian Unions in universities and colleges throughout the United Kingdom and the Republic of Ireland, and a member movement of the International Fellowship of Evangelical Students. For information about local and national activities write to UCCF, 38 De Montfort Street, Leicester LE1 7GP.

CONTENTS

FOREWORD

In a day when conflicting styles of leadership are hotly debated among Christians, Chua Wee Hian's new book contributes a much-needed perspective of biblical exposition to this vital subject.

A powerful and cogent explanation of scriptural principles and priorities, this book is enriched by a wealth of personal experience, practical advice, warm, down-to-earth humour and illustration.

No Christian called to leadership, whether in a student group, a local church or Christian organization, experienced or novice, could fail to benefit from this challenging yet sensitive statement of the Bible's neglected teaching on one of today's most misunderstood subjects. Buy it for your pastor or your church officers; it's a delight to read!

David Jackman
Minister of Above Bar Church, Southampton

INTRODUCTION

One of my favourite pastimes at airports is to look at the books that are for sale on their bookstalls. Romantic novels, spy-thrillers and science fiction invariably occupy prominent shelves. In recent months, however, books on leadership and management have commanded prime space.

Prospective customers are tantalized by titles and blurbs on book covers which promise to reveal the secrets or inside stories of successful industrialists, entrepreneurs, generals and politicians. These eminent men and women tell their stories to ghost-writers. The plot is often simple and straightforward. They recount the odds stacked against them at the start of their careers and how they floundered when they approached their tasks according to the traditional patterns of management. They couldn't motivate people, they failed to reach their goals, and if they were in the world of commerce, their sales figures were pathetic. But then something 'miraculous' happened when they latched onto a particular formula or approach. In their scrupulous application of these new-found principles, they discovered that they could surmount obstacles, rivalry and competition. They reached the pinnacle of success and were now basking in the sunshine of fame and recognition.

Their books have a moral for readers: 'Follow my style of leadership or my recipe for success and you too will reach the top!' People willingly part with their money because they are curious to discover how these principles actually work and what makes these celebrities tick. Perhaps they are also thinking of their own situations: some are yearning to improve their managerial skills; others are ambitious and want to scale the ladder of promotion. These books on leadership hold out the promise that all those who read them and apply some of the methods described will become more effective leaders and managers.

The Christian church today is also fascinated by the subject of effective leadership. Here in the west, Christian publishers are churning out numerous books on this theme. Some authors despair over churches and Christian organizations that simply run and repeat programmes year in year out without any clear objectives. They rarely stop to review their activities and goals. So these writers seek to awaken the semi-deaf army of volunteers by beating the drum of sound and efficient organization. They are keen to get across the message of wholesome management principles so that Christian fellowships will become more effective in their service and outreach. The rediscovery of spiritual gifts and every-member ministry leads some writers to attack the one-man-band approach to leadership. They maintain that there is a vast untapped reservoir of potential among lay people, who should be encouraged to exercise their talents in direct spiritual ministry. As we read their books, we come across chapters and charts that help us to identify our own gifts. At the same time, they offer leaders 'know-how' on simple principles of management such as setting goals, implementing objectives, delegating tasks, writing job descriptions and understanding the dynamics of working as a team.

Now these books on Christian leadership have tremendous value and they are written to redress particular areas of weakness in our churches and Christian organizations. They are profitable to read and we like finding out how we can solve certain organizational problems and picking up useful hints on planning. But many assume a certain framework of operations and the availability of paid staff and up-to-date office equipment.

An African pastor friend of mine was recently flown at great expense to the United States to attend two seminars on leadership. He showed me the files of material that he had collected and the books on Christian leadership and management that he had purchased. But he lamented rather ruefully, 'I don't see how I could possibly streamline and run my church in Kenya in that way. I don't even have a secretary! If I were to try to implement the things I have learnt, it would mean retraining my members to function as mid-west American church-goers!' Being a sharp theologian, he went on to make the point that some of these Christian books on leadership were simply echoing secular books on management and 'baptizing' certain principles with proof texts from Scripture. That led us to ask a rather primary question: Is there a *biblical agenda* for leadership? Or to put it another way, are there timeless principles of spiritual leadership that are valid for all cultures? In the training of leaders, do we simply teach them skills and make them aware of the dynamics of corporate leadership, or is there more to it than that?

Over the years, I have been invited to speak at conferences and consultations for leaders in every continent. I have always been stimulated by these sessions with pastors, missionaries, student workers, student leaders and lay leaders. I have tried to allow God's Word to set the agenda on this crucial subject of spiritual leadership. Often we have been amazed by the ways in which biblical insight and patterns of leadership have challenged our own styles and assumptions about leading God's people.

Learning to lead is an attempt to look at the biblical perspective of Christian leadership. Much of the material originally formed part of expositions and talks. I have been encouraged to set it down in writing by the feedback that I have been receiving from leaders in different parts of the world. My prayer is that when you read these chapters, you will think through them and check the principles expounded with the Scriptures. It is essential that we learn to lead God's people in his way, and with his wisdom and strength.

Acknowledgments

Writing a book these days can no longer be a private enterprise. I am indebted to a host of colleagues and friends who have helped me in the writing of this book.

First, I would like to thank the International Fellowship of Evangelical Students for granting me four months' sabbatical to read, reflect and write on the theme of leadership.

My personal secretary, Miss Sarah Dudley-Smith, has faithfully transcribed numerous tapes, helped with basic research and was fully involved in the revision of the original drafts.

I am also grateful to my wife, King Ling, and to our three sons, Andrew, Daniel and Stephen, for their encouragement and suggestions. They have helped me to improve my presentation in several chapters.

Dr Sue Brown, IFES Training Secretary, kindly found time in her busy life to read through the manuscript, and offered invaluable advice.

Finally, I would also like to thank the editorial team of Inter-Varsity Press for their encouragement and patience in working with me over this manuscript.

Chapter One

PORTRAITS OF LEADERSHIP: SERVANTS

Imagine you had been asked to design the cover for this book. What picture or symbols would you have used to convey the idea of leadership?

In 1981 I was in Brazil, conducting a series of workshops on spiritual leadership. The participants were mainly Brazilian students who were leaders of their Christian fellowships. At our first meeting I asked them to design a crest or logo on leadership. The best design was going to be immortalized on a tee-shirt. They came back with various emblems illustrating crowns, sceptres, shields, swords, lion heads and scrolls. There was a regal quality in all the motifs. I was impressed by the stamp of authority which was so evident in their handiwork. The winning design would proudly grace a tee-shirt and there would be no shortage of buyers!

These student leaders did not consult a thesaurus. I did. Under 'leadership' the synonyms included: authority, control, administration, effectiveness, superiority, supremacy, skill, capacity and power. I cast my eye at the word 'leader'. The list was most impressive: general, commander, director, manager, head, officer, captain, master, chieftain, governor, ruler, executive, boss and brains. Both lists dovetailed with the crests produced by the students.

We then studied Luke 22:24–27:

Also a dispute arose among them as to which of them was considered to be greatest. Jesus said to them, 'The kings of

13

the Gentiles lord it over them; and those who exercise authority over them call themselves Benefactors. But you are not to be like that. Instead, the greatest among you should be like the youngest, and the one who rules like the one who serves. For who is greater, the one who is at the table or the one who serves? Is it not the one who is at the table? But I am among you as one who serves.'

The disciples were at it again! There they were on the eve of Christ's crucifixion, arguing about who would be the greatest. They were expecting Jesus the Messiah to inaugurate a new kingdom. Naturally they wanted to bag the plum posts. But Jesus must have shattered their dreams and silenced their quarrel with these incisive words: ' "The kings of the Gentiles lord it over them; and those who exercise authority over them call themselves Benefactors. But you are not to be like that" ' (verses 25–26).

The servant-Lord

There is a striking contrast between worldly leadership and spiritual leadership. Christ knew that political rulers wielded immense power. Their subjects had to submit to their authority. As leaders, they could throw their weight around. But at the same time, they craved popularity. They wanted to play the role of benefactors, so they liberally dispensed privileges. One thing is clear: leaders formed the apex of the hierarchical pyramid.

' "But you are not to be like that." ' In God's kingdom there is a radically new pattern of leadership: the first serve. Leadership is servanthood.

To reinforce this new order, Jesus asked this question: ' "For who is greater, the one who is at the table or the one who serves? Is it not the one who is at the table?" ' (verse 27). No marks for the right answer! The guest at a banquet and the patron in a restaurant are treated with honour. They are attended by waiters. The privileged guests breathe the air of greatness.

You can almost hear the hush as Jesus announced, ' "But I

14

am among you as one who serves" ' (verse 27). He assumed the role of a servant. Christ is the servant-Lord, and this is not a contradiction in terms. He uttered these unforgettable words, ' "For even the Son of Man did not come to be served, but to serve, and to give his life as a ransom for many" ' (Mark 10:45).

The Fourth Gospel records for us the moving scene of Jesus washing the feet of his disciples:

> Jesus knew that the Father had put all things under his power, and that he had come from God and was returning to God; so he got up from the meal, took off his outer clothing, and wrapped a towel round his waist. After that, he poured water into a basin and began to wash his disciples' feet, drying them with the towel that was wrapped around him (John 13:3–5).

Here the Lord Jesus undertook the role of the lowest slave. It was an act of love and humility. The dusty, dirty feet of his disciples needed washing. But there was no house-slave around so Jesus performed the task. How embarrassing! We can almost see the dozen red faces as he knelt to wash their feet.

What an unforgettable visual lesson on service and humility! But it wasn't just an acted parable. Christ reminded the Twelve:

> 'Do you understand what I have done for you? . . . You call me "Teacher" and "Lord", and rightly so, for that is what I am. Now that I, your Lord and Teacher, have washed your feet, you also should wash one another's feet. I have set you an example that you should do as I have done for you . . . Now that you know these things, you will be blessed if you do them' (verses 12–15, 17).

Jesus has established once and for all the foundation of spiritual leadership. The essence of leadership is service. Spiritual leaders are called to serve God and his people. This is non-negotiable. Christian leaders are expected to put this into practice: ' "You will be blessed if you do them" ' (verse 17).

Emblems of leadership

After studying these passages, the Brazilian students had to redesign their crests and logos. The revised versions incorporated the ordinary symbols of a towel and a basin of water, or figures kneeling in service. But we faced a problem. Suppose these emblems of service and humility were transferred to tee-shirts, how many people would have purchased and worn one? Would you?

Leaders as servants

The apostle Paul is universally recognized by Christians as an outstanding leader in Christ's church. But in his life and ministry he repeatedly described himself as a bond-slave of Jesus Christ.

We know that Paul was a Roman citizen and he took pride in his citizenship (see Acts 16:37–38). He rejoiced in his freedom. Yet he deliberately chose the word *doulos* to describe his position. He was Christ's bond-slave (*e.g.* Romans 1:1; Philippians 1:1; Titus 1:1). Paul had been commissioned by the risen Christ to be an apostle. He was invested with spiritual authority (see Romans 1:1, 5; Galatians 1:1). He established numerous churches and was one of the recognized leaders of the infant church. And yet he wanted everyone to know that he was a slave of Jesus Christ. He had no rights. All he was and all he had were at his Master's disposal. Thus his ministry was always Christ-centred (*e.g.* Philippians 1:20–21). He was eager that he and his team members should always be regarded as servants of Jesus Christ.

I have preached in many churches and chapels in England. One popular text which is often inscribed on the main wall of evangelical churches, usually behind the pulpit, is 2 Corinthians 4:5. In most cases only half the verse is quoted: 'We preach Jesus Christ as Lord' – the central proclamation of our faith.

Now if there was limited wall space, we could understand the reason for only painting six words. But most church walls are massive! The full text reads:

> For we do not preach ourselves, but Jesus Christ as Lord,
> and ourselves as your servants for Jesus' sake.

Christ is the main subject and object of our preaching. We are
not to draw attention to ourselves. At the same time, however,
our text clearly tells us that there should be a double proclamation – preaching Christ, and also 'preaching ourselves as
servants (Greek *doulous*) for Jesus' sake'. The full text
combines the Lordship of Christ and the servanthood of his
representatives. If our proclamation of Christ as Lord is backed
up by our ministry as servants, the gospel will spread more
effectively.

I find it relatively easy to pay lip-service to the concept of
leaders as bond-slaves of Christ. But we live in a generation
that glories in rights. We are taught to fight for our independence. We prefer to be our own bosses. In practice it is very
difficult to hand over all we are and have to Jesus Christ.

My predecessor, the late Mr C. Stacey Woods, loved to
tell the story about Dr Alexander Clarke. He was a medical
missionary who worked in the Belgian Congo, as it was then
called. One day he and a party of hospital attendants went
hunting in the jungle. They entered a clearing just in time
to see a lion attacking and mauling an African. Dr Clarke
immediately raised his rifle, took aim, pulled the trigger and
shot the lion. He and his men carried the wounded African
back to the mission hospital where he received urgent medical
attention and surgery. After a few weeks of recuperation he
returned to his village on the other side of the mountains.

Several weeks later, Dr Clarke was sitting on the verandah
of his bungalow when he heard a great commotion. There was
a cacophony of noise – the bleating of sheep and goats, and
the clucking and clacking of hens and ducks. He also heard the
loud chatter of human voices. Then he saw the princely figure
of an African leading a long procession of poultry, animals,
young children, and men and women carrying their possessions
on their heads.

Dr Clarke recognized the African. He was none other than
the man he had saved from the lion. The man ran towards
the doctor and prostrated himself at his feet. Then he spoke:

'According to the law of our tribe, a man who has been rescued from the jaws of a wild beast no longer belongs to himself; he belongs to his rescuer.' He stood up and went on: 'All that I have is yours. My hens and ducks, sheep and goats, my servants, my children, my wives and myself – all are yours. You are *bwana* (the chief) and I am your slave.'

The phrase, 'a man who has been rescued from the jaws of a wild beast no longer belongs to himself; he belongs to his rescuer', has a familiar ring. It echoes the words of the apostle: 'You are not your own; you were bought at a price. Therefore honour God with your body' (1 Corinthians 6:19b–20). When we appreciate Christ as our redeemer-rescuer and his great love in dying for us, we nail our rights to his cross. With gratitude, we hand our lives and our gifts to him and commit ourselves unreservedly to his service. Leadership begins at the foot of the cross. And our continuing motivation to serve Christ and others is governed by our understanding of Christ's death and by the time we spend 'at the cross'.

Servants – for ministry

Another popular Greek word which is translated as 'servant' is *diakonos*. This word occurs some thirty times in the New Testament, and its cognates *diakoneō* (to minister) and *diakonia* (ministry or service) are used in a further seventy references. Originally *diakonos* was used of a table-waiter or servant. The service rendered by Martha or Peter's mother-in-law is described as *diakonia* (see Luke 10:40; Mark 1:31). In a passage which we considered earlier (Luke 22:27), our Lord described himself as a table-waiter. The stress is on practical service or ministry.

This concept of ministry is underscored in the appointment of the seven to distribute food to the Greek-speaking widows in the Jerusalem church (see Acts 6). It does not equate leadership simply with privileges and authority. It is functional. Leaders are commissioned to serve others. The only sense of privilege stems from God's gracious calling. Writing of his own ministry, the apostle Paul stressed that his leadership responsibility was not based on self-commendation or references from dignitaries

(2 Corinthians 3:1). He asserted that it was God who 'made us competent as ministers of a new covenant – not of the letter but of the Spirit; for the letter kills, but the Spirit gives life' (verse 6). This awesome privilege should create in us the right spirit in which to serve others in the fellowship of the church.

Servants, not superstars

The church at Corinth had the wrong view of leadership. The promotion of personality cults had led to quarrels and divisions in the church (1 Corinthians 1:11–12). Some Christians idolized Paul. After all, he had founded their church and was a spiritual father to many of them (4:15). A second group rooted for Apollos. They were captivated by his systematic and intellectual preaching. Apollos came from the university centre of Alexandria, and was a powerful apologist. The third party preferred Peter. Wasn't he the chief apostle? To them he embodied the conservative element of the church – Paul and Apollos were radicals by comparison! This group was eager to observe customs and tradition and to be ruled by the letter of the law. Then there was an extraordinary fourth party – 'the Christ party'. Its members were hyper-spiritual. Instead of working for their unity in Christ, they made Christ a party leader. They waved his banner and made themselves out to be by far the best party.

How did the apostle resolve the divisions in the church? How did he deal a death-blow to the shameful personality cults which the Corinthians had created?

Theologically, Paul first reminded them of their unity in Christ. Their allegiance was to Christ crucified, not to any human leader (1:13). But Paul did not stop there. He was anxious that the Corinthian Christians should be taught how to view and relate to their leaders.

He castigated them for their immaturity and their worldly way of treating leaders (3:1–4). Jealousy, quarrelling and the promoting of personality cults are all out of keeping with Christian conduct. They were acting as 'mere men' and not following the way of Christ. Paul went on to employ a rather derogatory pronoun to describe Apollos and himself. Instead of saying,

'*Who*, after all, is Apollos? And *who* is Paul?', he deliberately chose the neuter pronoun 'what', as if to say, '*What thing* is Apollos or Paul?' (see verse 5).

Then he gave his definitive answer: 'Only servants, through whom you came to believe' (verse 5). They were simply the agents of their salvation – not the objects of their faith, or Paul would have said, '*in* whom you came to believe'.

Paul explained that God assigns different tasks to his servants (verses 5–9). Paul planted the gospel seed. Apollos watered it. But it was God who made it grow. The servants played their part in the Corinthian harvest, but only the Lord himself could produce spiritual life. The amazing thing was that he chose to work through his servants Paul, Apollos and Peter. We too are '*God's fellow-workers*' (verse 9). Ultimately we are responsible to him, and he is the one who will reward us for our labour (verse 8).

Willingness to work under others

To ram his point home, Paul concluded his argument with these words: 'So then, men ought to regard us as *servants* of Christ and as those entrusted with the secret things of God' (1 Corinthians 4:1). The word translated 'servant' in this particular text is not *doulos* or *diakonos*. Rather, it is the colourful term *huperetes*, which literally means 'under-rower'. In apostolic times, slaves were employed to row large galleys across the Mediterranean Sea. It was hard work in hot and dirty conditions, and they had to obey the commands of their overseers. They were totally under the authority of their masters.

Leaders love to rule the roost. We will gladly assume responsibility as the senior pastor, general secretary, director or president. But it requires humility to serve in a team or to take on a 'lower position'. Paul wanted the Corinthian Christians to think of him and Apollos as under-rowers – those who were prepared to do the menial tasks and to submit to the authority of other Christian leaders.

A close look at ourselves

We need to ask ourselves whether our pattern of leadership reflects the biblical portrait of servanthood, or whether we are being squeezed into the world's mould.

The spirit of the age often creeps into the arena of spiritual leadership. In the quest for excellence and efficiency, churches and Christian organizations can unconsciously create a 'superstar' image of their leaders. Christian books and magazines have coined a new term for pastors of mega-churches and the chief officers of Christian organizations: 'the Christian executive'. Christian executives dress in a certain style, travel on luxury airlines and drive exclusive cars. Even their offices are designed by specialists.

One of my friends became the director of a large Christian relief agency. He wasn't the tallest of 'executives', being only five feet six inches in height. His operations committee replaced the existing secretary who was five feet eight inches tall with someone who was five feet three! What mattered most was his public image; he must not be 'dwarfed' by his assistant.

Superstar leaders have the power to hire and fire. Their churches and organizations are run by teams of professionals. Those who make the grade receive high salaries and expenses. Those who fail are relegated to the sidelines.

When I was in California, I happened to be present when the board chairman of a large church offered a friend of mine the post of senior pastor. He refused, explaining that he had a contract to honour with his present church. 'That's no problem!' announced the chairman in his broad Texan drawl, 'I'll take care of that. Ask your church board to name a price and we'll pay.' I was flabbergasted. My friend just shook his head in disbelief. He was being treated like a football star and the board chairman was even prepared to negotiate a high transfer fee so that the pastor could break his contract with his church.

Some exponents of rapid church-growth theories advocate the strategy of appointing a *caudillo*-type pastor – a strong and powerful leader whom everyone looks up to. His word is law. Committees are a waste of time. He never beats about the bush but acts swiftly. He guarantees an increase in numbers. Unfortunately many Christians love being led by such an authoritarian leader. They let him set the direction and pace. For their part, they offer adulation and total obedience.

If we allow our leadership to be shaped by that school of management, what room is there for mutual submission (see Ephesians 5:21)? What about accountability to the Lord and to one another, which is the hallmark of servant-leadership? In promoting leaders to the premier league of superstars, are we not falling into the same trap as the Corinthians? Moreover, the leadership of these men can only thrive with the unquestioning support of their followers. Are rank-and-file Christians simply called to be loyal backers of an ecclesiastical superstar? How do we reconcile this with the biblical teaching and practice of using our different gifts and talents to build up the body of Christ?

Our standing as servants poses a daily challenge to 'walk humbly' with our God (Micah 6:8b). He has no room for proud and arrogant leaders. When we serve him with a sincere heart, we will not boast of our gifts and talents. Neither will we glory in spiritual experiences because we recognize that all blessings come from God. Humble leaders constantly rely on God. We should not go our own way. Rather, we need the injunction of Proverbs 3:6: 'In all your ways acknowledge him, and he will make your paths straight.' This means prayerful dependence. We must avoid the pitfall of thinking that we can solve every problem and achieve every goal by ourselves. Our humility should enable us to take our cue from the Lord:

> As the eyes of slaves look to
> the hand of their master,
> as the eyes of a maid look to
> the hand of her mistress,
> so our eyes look to the LORD
> our God,
> till he shows us his mercy (Psalm 123:2).

It is often difficult to accept the servant's place.

A student leader is wondering how to spend a particular

evening. He could invite a struggling young Christian round for coffee. This would involve listening patiently to his questions and problems. He is aware that this brother needs a bit of help and encouragement. On the other hand, he could spend the evening with three of his fellow committee members. He always enjoys their company and finds their conversation stimulating.

What does he do? First he prays. Then as he reflects on biblical principles, he hears afresh Christ's command to his disciples to minister to others. The young Christian needs his love and attention. So he lays aside self-interest and goes to find him. In so doing, he experiences what it means to have the mind and attitude of Christ in serving others (see Philippians 2:3–8).

Servants, but also friends

As a summary of what we have considered so far, and as a prelude to the next two chapters, let us take a look at the following chart, drawn up by George Mallone of Canada (Mallone 1981:86).

Secular Authority 'Lord Over'	Servant Authority 'Servant Among'
power base	love/obedience base
gives orders	under orders
unwilling to fail	unafraid/model of transformation
absolutely necessary	expendable
drives like a cowboy	leads like a shepherd
needs strength to subject	finds strength in submission
authoritarian	steward of authority
has gold, makes rules	follows golden rule
seeks personal advancement	seeks to please master
expects to be served	expects to serve

In serving Christ, we shall discover that he doesn't remain aloof. Nor does he simply issue orders for us to obey or treat us as errand boys. As we serve him, he surprises us! He encourages us to cultivate a new depth of relationship with him by inviting us to be his friends and confidants. 'You are my friends', Jesus said, 'if you do what I command. I no longer call you servants, because a servant does not know his master's business. Instead, I have called you friends . . .' (John 15:14–15). As his companions, he shares his plans and secrets with us. We are in royal company: there is joy and nobility in being his servant-friends.

Chapter Two

PORTRAITS OF LEADERSHIP: STEWARDS

The second set of portraits in the biblical gallery of leadership depicts stewards. Some modern English versions of the Bible translate *oikonomos* (Greek for steward) as 'manager' and *oikonomia* (Greek for stewardship) as 'management' (see Luke 12:42; 16:1–3). Today we associate the profession of stewards and stewardesses with the employees of airlines or ships who attend to the needs of passengers. In Britain, stewards are officers who monitor competitions such as Grand Prix motor-racing and horse-racing. But the Greek word *oikonomos* literally means a house-manager. In New Testament times, wealthy householders employed stewards to supervise servants and to manage their domestic affairs. Stewards were normally slaves, but they had earned the respect and trust of the householders, who had in turn promoted them to positions of responsibility.

As we consider the biblical portrayal of leadership, I would like to emphasize the image of the steward. It highlights the responsibilities of spiritual leaders.

Stewards as trustees

First, stewards serve as trustees. J. B. Phillips translates 'stewards' as 'trustees' in 1 Corinthians 4:1. The NIV amplifies this word-picture, describing them as 'those entrusted with the secret things of God'.

The position of trustee brings with it the twin sense of privilege and responsibility. The apostle Paul was very conscious of his privileged standing. He was entrusted with the 'administration [literally 'stewardship'] of God's grace' (Ephesians 3:2). This stewardship was associated with a mystery, the mystery of Christ (verses 3–5). The apostle was excited that God had delivered a special secret to him.

Now we normally associate the word 'mystery' with puzzles or riddles. The Greek word *mystērion* has nothing to do with hidden secrets into which devotees of popular mystery religions had to be initiated. The mystery referred to in the New Testament is God's open secret which he had revealed to the church. John Stott makes this perceptive comment:

> Originally, the Greek word referred to a truth into which someone had been initiated. Indeed it came to be used of the secret teachings of the heathen mystery religions, teachings which were restricted to initiates. But in Christianity there are no 'esoteric' mysteries reserved for a spiritual élite. On the contrary, the Christian 'mysteries' are truths which, although beyond human discovery, have been revealed by God and so now belong openly to the whole church (Stott 1979:116).

Paul rejoiced in the privilege of sharing God's open secrets with both Gentiles and Jews. They were 'heirs together', 'members together of one body' and 'sharers together . . . in Christ Jesus' (Ephesians 3:6). These precious truths had been 'revealed by the Spirit to God's holy apostles and prophets' (verse 5). It was through God's sheer love and grace that Paul was entrusted 'to preach to the Gentiles the unsearchable riches in Christ' (verse 8).

With privilege comes responsibility. Paul was so gripped by this glorious gospel that he was prepared to deny all his rights so that he could proclaim it widely (see 1 Corinthians 9:16–18). He felt keenly the weight of this responsibility: 'Woe to me if I do not preach the gospel!' (verse 16).

Being a trustee of God's good news, he had to discharge his obligation to preach to both Jews and Gentiles (Romans 1:14). With deep assurance he stated, 'I am not ashamed of the gospel, because it is the power of God for the salvation of everyone who believes: first for the Jew, then for the Gentile' (verse 16). Every leader should be thrilled by the privilege of being a trustee of the gospel. God has committed to us a dynamic message which can transform lives. As men and women respond to God's free offer of salvation in Christ, their sins are blotted out, their guilt forgiven, and they enter into a new relationship with the living God.

But we can be irresponsible trustees. Instead of planning ways of sharing this good news with others, we can waste precious hours discussing and dissecting it to make it fit into our neat theological pigeon-holes. Meanwhile, hundreds of people remain in darkness, without God and without hope, and as trustees of the gospel we are accountable to God. He will hold us responsible if we neglect to share his love and power with others.

Stewards as guardians

Second, stewards are guardians. Paul pressed his younger colleague Timothy, 'Guard the good deposit that was entrusted to you – guard it with the help of the Holy Spirit who lives in us' (2 Timothy 1:14).

This 'good deposit' refers to the gospel and the apostolic faith (see verses 8, 13). It is a priceless treasure. We are to defend it with our lives. We are to prevent God's enemies from invading and robbing us of this treasure. Being custodians doesn't mean that we should construct a line of defence to protect the gospel treasure. The apostolic faith has to be propagated, and this often leads to conflict. Others will challenge its validity and authenticity. So we need to 'contend for the faith that was once entrusted to the saints' (Jude 3).

Leaders today need to have clear biblical and theological convictions. We must never allow the apostolic faith to be watered down or compromised. We must always be valiant for truth. Critics will cast doubts on God's Word. Some will query its relevance to this age. Our task is to proclaim the truth and expose error so that God's people may be built up in their faith. This is the duty of leaders as the guardians of God's truth.

27

Stewards as transmitters of apostolic teaching

Third, stewards are transmitters of apostolic teaching. Towards the end of his life, the apostle Paul was eager for Timothy to pass on his teaching to other reliable teachers. Let us listen to his stirring words in 2 Timothy 2:2:

> And the things you have heard me say in the presence of many witnesses entrust to reliable men who will also be qualified to teach others.

Christian leaders do not only guard the apostolic truth: they must ensure its transmission.

This truth, like the baton in a relay race, must be handed on from one generation of leaders to the next. We must recruit, encourage and train others who will in turn teach and pass on God's revealed Word. The greatest tragedy is when a good work ends or dies with a particular leader. Success without a successor is failure.

Stewards as managers

Fourth, stewards are involved in management. God expects us to plan and organize things for his people. This is reflected in one of Jesus' cogent sayings:

> 'Who then is the faithful and wise steward, whom his master will set over his household, to give them their portion of food at the proper time? Blessed is that servant whom his master when he comes will find so doing' (Luke 12:42–43, RSV).

The master appoints the steward to manage his household. As leaders we cannot abdicate our God-given responsibility to ensure that God's people are properly fed. And we need to think of ways and means whereby they can use their spiritual gifts.

It is vital that we first take time to pray and then plan how to utilize the resources available to foster growth in his

28

kingdom. We can't avoid the over-all responsibility of managing God's people. Some might protest, 'What if you haven't got administrative gifts? I'm a hopeless organizer!' But God has endowed his people with different gifts so some will have gifts of administration (see 1 Corinthians 12:28). We can recruit the help of these men and women in our management tasks. Together we can set God-given directives and goals. We can take stock of our resources and, with God's enabling, seek to fulfil his plans for our church or fellowship. Someone has said, 'People never plan to fail. They simply fail to plan.' Failure to plan is an abuse of our role as managers.

Stewardship qualities

So far, we have considered the *functions* of stewards as trustees, guardians, transmitters of the faith and managers. Stewards also require certain essential *qualities*.

What are some of these qualities? In his letter to another of his prominent workers, Titus, the apostle Paul gave this guideline:

> For a bishop, as God's *steward*, must be blameless (Titus 1:7, RSV, emphasis mine).

In the Pastoral Epistles, the word *episkopos* (here translated 'bishop') means 'overseer'. Originally, its use was limited to those who exercised leadership in the local church (Guthrie 1961:79). Here we have a stringent quality expected of the church leader. He must possess an 'unimpeachable character' (verse 7, NEB). High moral standards are expected. Paul went on to declare, 'Rather he [the spiritual leader] must be hospitable, one who loves what is good, who is self-controlled, upright, holy and disciplined' (verse 8). We shall be considering these qualities in further detail in chapter 5.

Stewards are also expected to be *trustworthy* and *faithful* (Luke 12:42; see 1 Corinthians 4:2). No house-owner would leave his family and estate in the hands of his manager for a long period of time if he had suspicions about the man's trustworthiness.

The Lord requires us to be faithful in exercising our stewardship. We shouldn't let others down. When we promise to attend a meeting or perform a specific task, unless there are exceptional reasons we should deliver the goods. A faithful leader is one who has no credibility gap. His word is his bond. He discharges his responsibilities with a clear conscience.

Our Lord also contrasted the faithful and wise steward with the unfaithful and irresponsible one. The latter abused his privileges by exploiting his fellow servants and getting drunk. When his master turned up unexpectedly, the steward was severely punished (Luke 12:45ff.). Christ holds us accountable for the way in which we discharge our stewardship responsibilities. We care for God's people so we cannot be a law unto ourselves.

The Lord entrusts us, as stewards, with immense resources. He equips us with leadership gifts. How solemn then are the words of the Master:

'Every one to whom much is given, of him will much be required; and of him to whom men commit much they will demand the more' (Luke 12:48, RSV).

Chapter Three

PORTRAITS OF LEADERSHIP: SHEPHERDS

An artist would probably paint rather austere portraits of servants and stewards. If he were to dwell on the idea of duty, he might portray them as faceless and obedient employees. A contemporary painter could easily develop the fashionable theme of excellence in leadership. His sketches of stewards might show characters exuding a rather cold competence and cultivated charm, working in clinically clean offices. However, in any painting of a shepherd, his weather-beaten face reflects care and concern for his flock. You cannot paint a shepherd by himself – you will always find him with his sheep. This portrait evokes warmth and intimacy.

The eastern shepherd

The eastern shepherd, as portrayed in the Bible, is different from his western counterpart. The former spends considerable time with the flock. You will always see him walking in front of his sheep (see Psalm 23:2; John 10:3–4). By contrast, I visited a farm in Raglan, New Zealand, and was treated to an unforgettable display of 'Kiwi' shepherding skills. To my amazement, the shepherds wore Levi jeans and rode on Honda motorbikes! With the aid of two barking sheepdogs they rounded up the sheep and drove them into the enclosure.

New Zealand has over seventy million sheep and only three million people. Understandably, the shepherds need high-powered bikes to assist them in their work. But this is a far cry from the oriental shepherd who sometimes spends day and night with his flocks (see Luke 2:8).

The Lord is my shepherd

Whenever we think of leaders as shepherds, our minds naturally race back to Psalm 23, which many of us know by heart. It begins with the reassuring statement, 'The Lord is my shepherd, I shall not want' (verse 1, RSV). Perhaps you have heard of the nervous schoolgirl who was struck by stage-fright when reciting this psalm. She blurted out, 'The Lord is my shepherd. That's all I want'! A genuine error, but it contained tremendous biblical insight! 'The Lord is my shepherd': it is a picture of intimacy and security. The sovereign Lord is no distant deity. He enters into a personal relationship with his people. As shepherd, the Lord provides food and rest for his sheep (verse 2). He refreshes and renews us; he leads us in prepared paths (verse 3). When we are wounded, he anoints our heads with oil (verse 5). No wonder his people testify to his goodness and mercy which accompany us on life's journey (verse 6).

Our hearts are further moved when we read the magnificent pastoral imagery used to describe our shepherd-Lord:

> He tends his flock like a
>   shepherd:
>   He gathers the lambs in his
>   arms
> and carries them close to his
>   heart;
>   he gently leads those that
>   have young (Isaiah 40:11).

Such is our God. He is a shepherd *par excellence*.

Good and bad shepherds

In Psalm 78:70–72, David is portrayed as the shepherd-king. He began life as the shepherd-boy, but God chose him to be his servant. The Mighty Shepherd had great plans for the young shepherd from Bethlehem. Before long he was anointed and crowned king. David's task was to shepherd God's people (verse 71), and he ably carried out his pastoral responsibilities. He had the right motivation for service – he 'shepherded them with integrity of heart' (verse 72). He was also a competent leader who led his people forward with skilful hands. Thus David reflected the shepherd qualities of the Great Shepherd himself.

By contrast, we are shown round a portrait gallery of bad shepherds. We see paintings of kings, political leaders and prophets who misguided God's people during the period before the exile. The prophet Ezekiel uttered strong words of denunciation:

'Woe to the shepherds of Israel who only take care of themselves! Should not shepherds take care of the flock? . . . you do not take care of the flock. You have not strengthened the weak or healed the sick or bound up the injured. You have not brought back the strays or searched for the lost. You have ruled them harshly and brutally. So they were scattered because there was no shepherd, and when they were scattered they became food for all the wild animals. My sheep wandered . . . They were scattered over the whole earth, and no-one searched or looked for them' (Ezekiel 34:2–6).

These leaders were terribly irresponsible. God would judge the shepherds and the ill-disciplined sheep which liked to butt and hurt other sheep (verses 7–10, 17–22). But out of love, the Lord himself was also planning to step in and rescue his people:

'I myself will search for my sheep and . . . gather them . . . I will tend them in a good pasture . . . I will bind up the injured and strengthen the weak' (verses 11–16).

The prophet looked ahead to the age of the Messiah when there would be 'one shepherd, my servant David, and he will tend them; he will tend them and be their shepherd' (verse 23). These prophetic words point to the person and ministry of Jesus, the Good Shepherd.

Jesus the Good Shepherd

It is fascinating to note that in rabbinical writing, the occupation of shepherd is bracketed with those of the hated publican and the tax-collector. Shepherds were despised as rogues and thieves. In fact, their testimony would not be admitted in a court of law (*Theological Dictionary of the New Testament* Vol. 6 1967:488–489).

The shepherds who heard the angels on the first Christmas Day probably suffered from this reputation. When Jesus compares himself to a shepherd, John stresses that he was *The* Shepherd – the *Good* Shepherd (John 10:11).

What can we learn from the picture of Jesus as the Good Shepherd? How can Christian leaders develop shepherd-like qualities? How are we meant to relate to God's people?

First, the shepherd knows each sheep by name (John 10:3, 14, 27). For Jesus, sheep are not all alike. He personally calls each one by name. Leaders have no excuse for saying, 'I am hopeless at remembering names.' If we are really concerned about people, the least we can do is remember their names.

Business corporations and commercial enterprises do all they can to inject a personal touch into their relationships with clients. A customer once wrote a letter of complaint to the manager of a large department store. His public relations secretary immediately typed a letter to pacify her. But the secretary must have had an off-day because the note ended, 'We would like to assure you, madam, that we fake an interest in every customer.' Striking the wrong key on a typewriter can make a fatal difference! The Lord's interest in his people is not faked; it is genuine. And he expects us to cultivate close personal relationships with those whom we serve.

Second, the shepherd is always with his sheep. He is available when they need him. Christ is not a remote shepherd-leader, who needs to be paged on some bleeper. Who can miss the beauty and the warmth of his words, 'I am *among* you as one who serves' (Luke 22:27b)? Spiritual leaders should always be approachable. We must get alongside our people if we are to know and serve them well.

Third, the shepherd leads the flock. Christ the Good

Shepherd always goes ahead of his sheep. He guides us to pastures and water-holes. Let your imagination capture the scene Jesus himself describes:

> 'He calls his own sheep by name and leads them out. When he has brought out all his own, he goes on ahead of them, and his sheep follow him . . . ' (John 10:3b–4).

The spectacle of an eastern shepherd going ahead of his sheep is still a common sight in Israel today. An Arab guide was once showing a group of tourists around the Holy Land. On one of their coach trips, he alluded to this tradition of the Palestinian shepherd walking in front of his flock. While he was speaking, the tourists spotted a man in the distance driving a small flock of sheep with a rather menacing stick. Just as all schoolchildren love to prove their teachers wrong, they pointed the figure out to the guide.

He immediately stopped the bus and rushed off across the fields. A few minutes later he returned, his face beaming. He announced, 'I have just spoken to the man. Ladies and gentlemen, he is not the shepherd. He is in fact the butcher!'

Spiritual leaders, like eastern shepherds, have to lead the way. Often we have to blaze the trail for God's people. We are expected to guide them to fresh pastures. We must direct people to God's Word and feed them by our teaching, and also teach them how to feed themselves from the Bible. Moreover, by going ahead of God's people we will be the first to smell danger so we can warn our people to beware of approaching wild beasts (a metaphor for false teachers and heretics).

Fourth, the shepherd displays a deep concern for those who are lost. Jesus told a simple parable of a shepherd who was prepared to leave ninety-nine of his sheep so he could look for one that had strayed (Matthew 18:12–14; Luke 15:4–6). His heart leapt with joy when he found the missing sheep. Leaders who don't possess a pastor's heart might question, 'What are a few lost sheep? Or backsliding Christians? Why spend precious time wooing them back? Let them find out for themselves the stupidity of leaving the fold.' In his earthly ministry, Christ associated with the social outcasts. He was dubbed 'a friend of tax collectors and "sinners" ' (Matthew 11:19). For him that was a compliment. Leaders today should always be in the business of searching for the lost sheep, that is, those who are alienated from God and need to be reconciled to him. We are also to restore those who have lost their bearings and have been side-tracked into the paths of sin.

Jesus was eager that his disciples, the future leaders of his kingdom, should see the multitudes through his eyes. For them, the crowd was simply a mass of people. For economists and sociologists, it would have been just another statistic. Jesus saw them differently: 'They were harassed and helpless, like sheep without a shepherd' (Matthew 9:36). He was deeply moved by what he saw: 'he had compassion on them'. His shepherd's heart sought to reach out to them. Using a different metaphor, Christ presented his disciples with another picture of the crowd: ' "The harvest is plentiful but the workers are few. Ask the Lord of the harvest, therefore, to send out workers into his harvest field" ' (verses 37–38).

Fifth, the shepherd protects the sheep. Sheep attract different kinds of predators. Wild beasts like wolves attack and kill. Birds of prey swoop on unsuspecting lambs and carry them off as food for their young. Thieves and robbers are bent on snatching them from the fold (John 10:10).

Christ also referred to another group of men: hirelings. They were paid to look after the flock, but in the face of danger they would abandon the sheep (verse 12). Why? Because they were only paid to do their job, so there was no intimate relationship between them and the sheep. The welfare of the flock was not uppermost in their minds (verse 13). By contrast, the Good Shepherd guards and cares for all the sheep. Spiritual shepherds are called to exercise oversight. One of our primary functions is to guard God's people from the frenzied attacks of false teachers. They seek to harm Christians by their poisonous teaching. As leaders we need to warn our members against the wiles of Satan (see Ephesians 6:11). We must teach them to put on the whole armour of God so that they can resist the assaults of the Evil One (verses 11–18). And we must expose sin in all its forms. We have terrific responsibility as guardians of God's flock.

Sixth, the shepherd is prepared to die for the sheep. In John 10, Jesus the Good Shepherd disclosed his willingness to lay down his life for the sheep (verses 11, 15, 17–18). This is the acid test of leadership. Do we love the people under our care so much that we are prepared to die for them? It is a sobering test.

In times of persecution, we hear moving reports of loyal pastors and Christian leaders who are prepared to go to prison and sometimes even to die in order to protect their members. One of the greatest phenomena of this age has been the growth of the church in China. In 1951, when all western missionaries were driven from the country, the Protestant church had a million members. The Marxist authorities confiscated church buildings and mission schools, and imprisoned leaders who refused to undergo the 'reforming' of their thought, a euphemism for indoctrination. Physical persecution rose to a new height during the Cultural Revolution (1966–75).

On one occasion the notorious Red Guards incited the local police to arrest the leaders of a particular house church. They raided the house and arrested the preacher on the spot. To their surprise, they were greeted with an unusual chorus of protest. The couple who owned the house asked the police to arrest them instead. The songleader pushed himself forward and declared that he was responsible for all the noise and music so he should be imprisoned. Other leaders implored the police to arrest them and free the others. In the end about a dozen people were imprisoned! Once behind bars, they began to witness to the other prisoners. The police concluded that they were more dangerous in prison than out, so released them!

Such stories could be multiplied. Through those fearless witnesses, and others like them, the church in China has grown beyond all expectations. Today, thirty-five years later, that church has around sixty million believers.

The picture of Christ as the Good Shepherd highlights the essential qualities of those called to be his under-shepherds. Like him, we are to cultivate a warm, personal relationship with the people we work with. We must be available to them. We are to guide and lead them forward. We should diligently seek the lost, sinners and backsliders. We must guard and

37

protect them. If necessary, we must be willing to die for them.

The fisherman who became a shepherd

Peter was a fisherman when he first met Jesus. Christ then called him to be one of the Twelve – he would no longer be catching fish, but men (Luke 5:10b)! The call of the sea and the nets is something innate in fishermen. After the resurrection, Peter and his companions were feeling rather restless, waiting for the risen Lord to appear to them again, so they decided to go fishing. But the expedition was a failure. They fished all night and caught nothing (John 21:3). When dawn appeared, they heard the voice of Jesus, 'Have you caught anything?' What an embarrassing question! He commanded them to throw their nets on the right side of the boat. Rather sceptically they did so and landed a huge catch. One hundred and fifty-three whoppers, to be precise! That took some beating! What a story to tell their friends!

When Peter and the others hauled in their catch, they discovered that Jesus had thoughtfully cooked breakfast for them. After their picnic, Jesus the Great Shepherd took Peter aside. Three times he asked his disciple, 'Do you love me?' Three times the apostle answered, 'Yes, you know that I love you' (verses 15–17). After each affirmation of Peter's love for him, Christ gave three clear commands: 'Feed my lambs', 'Take care of my sheep', and 'Feed my sheep'. It's true that he first called Peter to fish for men, but he also charged him to exercise the role of a shepherd-leader.

Christ calls leaders today to serve as his under-shepherds. He commissions us to feed his lambs, that is, younger Christians. C. H. Spurgeon reminded theological students that the Lord calls pastors to feed his lambs and sheep, not his giraffes! Preachers have no business to present abstract theology to their congregations. We are to feed Christians with the milk and meat of God's Word. It is our task to provide our people with a regular, balanced diet of biblical food. Christians will only grow if they are nourished by Scripture.

So how can we ensure that our members are well taught and grounded in God's Word? A diagram may help:

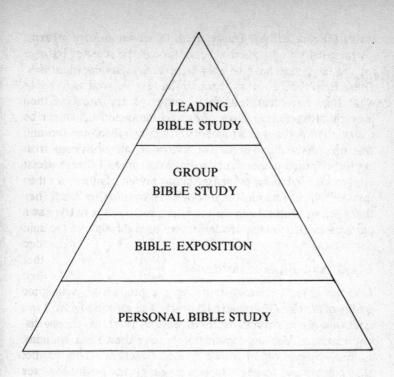

LEADING
BIBLE STUDY

GROUP
BIBLE STUDY

BIBLE EXPOSITION

PERSONAL BIBLE STUDY

Level one: personal Bible study

Our primary responsibility is to encourage and teach Christians to read the Bible for themselves. There is no substitute for daily, personal Bible study. We should press home the glorious truth that the living God meets with us through his written Word. Christians will then search the Scriptures with a deep sense of expectation.

We shouldn't assume that every young Christian knows how to read the Bible. Ideally, older Christians should spend time with younger ones, demonstrating how to read, understand and obey God's Word. We can introduce them to certain tools or aids, for example Bible dictionaries and commentaries. These will help them to understand the background of the Bible passages.

Personally, I encourage Christians to work through the whole Bible using the excellent study guide, *Search the Scriptures*

(IVP, UK and USA). I urge them to set aside forty minutes for their daily study. As they read through the selected passage for the day, they have to answer several searching questions. These help them to work through the text, as well as to apply what they have learnt to their contemporary situations. To prevent distraction, I have often recommended Christians to record their findings in a notebook. They can then pray through what they have discovered. The following questions help us to apply Scripture to our daily lives: What have I learnt about God today? What have I learnt about myself? Is there a sin to forsake? A commandment to obey? A warning to heed? Are there promises that I can claim? One good habit is to commit a particular verse to memory and reflect on it throughout the day.

Level two: Bible exposition

God has gifted leaders so that they can prepare his *people* for works of service (Ephesians 4:11–12). The ascended Christ has endowed some with the gifts of pastors (literally shepherds) and teachers. Various commentators have drawn our attention to the absence of an article before 'teachers'. This implies that pastors and teachers form a single group. Pastor-teachers should be faithful Bible expositors. They should be the ones who faithfully unfold and explain God's Word. They are not meant to ride their favourite hobby-horses, but rather to work through the texts and books of the Bible. They must avoid the temptation to take a text out of its context. They will faithfully seek to interpret texts or passages in their original settings and then apply their timeless truths to current situations and individual needs. It is through systematic preaching and teaching that God's people are nourished and built up.

Alas, too often preachers neglect the discipline of hard slog (expository preaching requires careful and thorough study) and impoverish themselves and their congregations. They may choose a different text each Sunday, but as one bored sermon critic put it:

Ten thousand thousand are their texts
But all their sermons one!

40

Not all leaders are Bible expositors. Not all are gifted teachers. But every spiritual leader is responsible for providing wholesome and basic spiritual food for his members. He may not be the expositor but it is his responsibility to ensure that someone is available to expound God's Word with clarity and power.

What if leaders cannot find Bible expositors? I encountered this problem when I was working with students in East Asia. All the staff that I spoke to agreed that we desperately needed Bible teachers. Popular preachers who could give pep devotional talks at the drop of a hat were two a penny. We also had our fair share of evangelists who could hold an audience spellbound while explaining the gospel to them. But we could count the number of good Bible teachers on the fingers of one hand!

So in the late sixties, our evangelical student movements in East Asia decided that we had to grow our own Bible expositors. In Taiwan, the staff team of the Campus Evangelical Fellowship embarked on a special study-training scheme. The staffworkers in Taipei came to the student centre every morning and devoted the first two hours of the day to uninterrupted study of God's Word and to prayer. They wouldn't even answer the telephone. Once a week, one of their number would expound a selected chapter or passage from Scripture. The others had all been studying the same passage and after about forty minutes of exposition, the team would analyse the sermon. They offered constructive criticism on both the content and presentation of the message. Thus a group of Bible teachers emerged.

Today, inexpensive cassettes of first-class Bible expositions are readily available, and budding expositors could profitably listen to these, or to sermons given by well-known teachers. Inter-Varsity Press has also published an outstanding series of contemporary commentaries called 'The Bible Speaks Today' series. These books contain model verse-by-verse expositions of various books of the Bible.

Young Christians in particular need to have an overview of God's plan and purpose as revealed in Scripture. Systematic exposition also introduces them to sound doctrine. This is essential for building up strong, mature and discerning Christians.

Level three: group Bible study

Ada Lum and Ruth Siemens once wrote, 'A group Bible study discussion is essentially a personal Bible study magnified . . . Group discussion may be defined as *cooperative thinking*' (Lum and Siemens 1973:15).

Group Bible studies can take place in an informal atmosphere and Christians will benefit from mutual learning and discovery. People learn best by participation, which is what group Bible study is all about. The group is committed to studying the set text. The leader will carefully frame questions that will provoke people to study the text thoroughly, think, raise questions and share their findings.

Here are some helpful guidelines for good and creative Bible studies. As in personal study, we need to *observe* the text. We should base our observation on facts. Then we have to *interpret* particular statements or events. What did the writer mean when he wrote that? What was the situation and environment of the original readers? What was the writer trying to get across to them? And then we need to *apply* the unchanging truths and principles to ourselves today. This requires bridge-building. The world of the Bible has to be bridged to the world of today. Christians are always surprised by the relevance of God's Word to present-day problems and situations.

The case of Adrian

Adrian was a good friend of mine. He was converted during his first year at university. I always remember Adrian for his tremendous hunger for God and his Word.

When I first met him, he had been a Christian for only six months. As I expounded the passage of Scripture, his eyes sparkled and I could sense him drinking in God's Word. Afterwards, he rushed up to me and said, 'Wow! What a great God we serve! It was mind-blowing to catch a glimpse of God's glory and grace in Isaiah 40' – the passage I had preached on that night. Later, over a cup of coffee, he spoke very warmly of his friend Bob. It was Bob who had prayed for him and taken him to the meeting where he had committed his life to Christ. For nearly a month, Bob had met with Adrian three times a week to study the Bible – 'He even taught me how to pray'. And Bob had taken him to a lively church where he could benefit greatly from the systematic Bible exposition.

Adrian was really excited about his personal Bible studies. He was using the Scripture Union notes which Bob had recommended. Then, in rather a charming and frank manner, he told me, 'I have been asked to lead the group Bible study in my home in two weeks' time. Will you please pray for me?' He had been assigned a passage from the first half of Philippians 4. Gillian, another member of his Christian Union, was going to act as an 'assistant leader'. She was an older Christian and promised that she would keep the discussion going if Adrian got stuck.

Two years later, I met Adrian at a student conference. I told him that I had remembered to pray for him and wondered how he had got on with the Bible study. 'It wasn't too bad. We had one or two red herrings. Someone kept arguing about the irreconcilable doctrines of predestination and human free will.' Apparently they had almost been side-tracked into a theological debate. But Gillian and others were able to steer the group back to observe the basic principle of discussing the text. Adrian mentioned that he had led a few more Bible studies since then. One could tell that he was growing by leaps and bounds. Yes, like everyone else he had had his share of problems and crises, but he had learnt to apply God's Word to his heart and life. He was allowing Scripture to shape his thinking and behaviour. The wonderful thing about him was his capacity to learn and to serve. And as he served, he grew.

Level four: discipling others

Christ commissioned us to make disciples of all nations (Matthew 28:19) and to teach them to observe all that he has commanded us (verse 20). Leaders are involved in disciple-making. Thinking ahead, we also need to mobilize others to take part in this crucial ministry.

Adrian set a fine example. One could see how his life had been changed through personal Bible study, Bible exposition and participating in group Bible studies. In his third year he was asked to lead an action group, which consisted of five other members. This group met weekly, and Adrian was expected to exercise pastoral care over each of the five. It was his task to motivate them to witness to their friends. Together they held evangelistic Bible studies where seekers could openly examine the claims of Christ. These provided splendid opportunities for Adrian to rally the action group members to pray for their non-Christian friends. They were thrilled when two of their friends became Christians.

Adrian allocated part of his busy schedule to nurture these young converts. One of them had come from a broken home. He had an enormous chip on his shoulder. It wasn't always easy to disciple him because of all his problems, but Adrian began to prove the power of God's Word in transforming the attitudes and relationships of this new Christian, and increasing his confidence in the Holy Spirit and in the Word of God.

One of our major tasks is to mobilize and equip people like Adrian to minister to others.

It was an historic gathering. The apostle Paul had summoned the elders or overseers in the Ephesian church to meet with him and his band of co-workers at the seaport of Miletus. There, in his stirring address, he unburdened his heart. He shared his aims and objectives. He also issued this charge to the Ephesian leaders:

'Guard yourselves and all the flock of which the Holy Spirit has made you overseers. Be shepherds of the church of God, which he bought with his own blood' (Acts 20:28).

He entreated them to exercise their ministry as shepherds or pastors, reminding them that their calling was one of immense privilege. Leaders are shepherds of God's redeemed people, called to exercise their leadership within the sphere of his church. This is no human institution: it is the church of God.

In order to be good shepherds, they first had to guard themselves. All leaders are vulnerable. We can be unfaithful. Satan will seek every opportunity to pounce on us and try to defeat us. So we must be vigilant. We must also protect God's people as this is part and parcel of our role as overseers.

We need to guard God's flock against heresy and falsehood. Developing the pastoral imagery, Paul warned the Ephesian elders of savage wolves that would ravage the flock. Heretics and false teachers would deny and distort God's truth. They would even have their own following (verses 29–31). So he issued his challenge: 'Be on your guard!'

Christian leaders have to combat heresies. Heretics who propound erroneous doctrines are often members of the church. How are we meant to deal with them? We must expose and refute them. Like the apostle, we should warn Christians to steer clear of any deviations or distortions of God's Word. Positively, we should obey the apostolic injunction to preach the whole will of God (verse 27) and never hesitate to 'preach anything that would be helpful' (verse 20). Only the proclamation of truth can dispel heresy.

Shepherds, servants and stewards

We have already referred to the memorable occasion when the Lord Jesus commissioned Peter to shepherd his people (see John 21:15–17). The theme of shepherding stuck in the apostle's mind. Many years after the event, Peter exhorted his fellow elders:

> Be shepherds of God's flock that is under your care, serving as overseers – not because you must, but because you are willing, as God wants you to be; not greedy for money, but eager to serve; not lording it over those entrusted to you, but being examples to the flock (1 Peter 5:2–3).

Shepherds serve: so too should we, with willingness and enthusiasm. Service should not be motivated by money. Leaders are not bosses: we are not to lord it over others. Instead we are to be examples – a theme that we will be considering in the next chapter.

We can also detect the picture of stewardship in the text. God's people are those that have been *entrusted* to us. We are therefore accountable to the Chief Shepherd – the Lord Jesus himself (verse 4). He is the one who will reward us for our labours. As we faithfully serve and shepherd God's people, we shall be discharging our stewardship.

Some years ago I visited the National Art Gallery in Taipei, Taiwan. Some of the finest Chinese paintings are housed in this gallery. As I looked at these magnificent paintings on silk scrolls, I could see on them the distinctive mark of imperial seals. The Chinese emperors used to have personal seals by which they showed their approval. The paintings were therefore national treasures. We are engaged in the task of leading, and of forming and shaping leaders. What patterns do we follow? How carefully do we study and emulate the biblical portraits of leadership? When our Lord and Master sees our work, will he give us his seal of approval?

May I suggest that you stop and reflect for a moment? You might like to pray for fellow leaders using the pastoral doxology at the end of the letter to the Hebrews:

> May the God of peace, who through the blood of the eternal covenant brought back from the dead our Lord Jesus, *that great Shepherd of the sheep*, equip you with everything good for doing his will, and may he work in us what is pleasing to him, through Jesus Christ, to whom be glory for ever and ever. Amen (Hebrews 13:20–21, emphasis mine).

Chapter Four

LEADERS AS EXAMPLES

All of us learn by example. When a five-year-old girl puts on high-heeled shoes and paints her face and finger-nails, she is simply imitating her mother. Children learn by watching.

A young couple were returning from their shopping expedition. The moment they opened their front door, they heard their nine-year-old son and seven-year-old daughter shouting at each other. Horrified, they rushed upstairs to try to stop the verbal battle. 'What's going on?' they exclaimed. But their son Mark just smiled. 'It's all right,' he said, 'Susan and I were simply playing father and mother'!

Children pick up the bad habits of adults. They are natural imitators. Few people are original thinkers. Edmund Burke (1729–97) once stated: 'Example is the school of mankind and they will learn from no other.' A Latin proverb reminds us that 'Example is better than precept'. Both statements may be exaggerated, but they contain more than a grain of truth.

Suppose you've never played tennis before and you decide to learn. What would you do? You could buy a racket and get hold of a 'Teach Yourself Tennis' book. Armed with your racket and manual, you attempt to learn the intricacies of serving. Then, fixing your eyes on the diagrams, you swing your racket to return imaginary shots. Finally, you summon up the courage to ask a friend for a game. You quickly discover your limitations!

But if you find someone to coach you, correcting your strokes, and showing you the best way to serve and return the ball, you will make good progress. Later, if you're really keen, you could return to those manuals. Their instructions will reinforce the practical lessons learnt on the court. We learn best by example and practice.

There is a striking similarity here to the ancient pattern of teaching. Unlike today, pupils did not spend endless hours in lecture rooms, nor did they read quantities of text-books. The world was their classroom. They tackled the problems of life. As pupils observed notable teachers like Socrates, Plato and Confucius in debate, they too began to appreciate their masters' philosophy and world view. Inspired by their masters' examples, they in turn adopted the same patterns in teaching others.

The same discipline applied to the training of skilled craftsmen. The ancient world did not have colleges for goldsmiths or painters. Young men gathered around professional craftsmen and artists, and learned as apprentices. First they had to watch their master at work. Then they were given simple assignments. As their skills increased they were allowed to work on intricate designs. Apprentices developed their skills through on-the-job training.

This pattern also applies to the training of spiritual leaders. We learn best by observing living examples. We may read treatises on humility and love, but when we watch at close quarters a person in whom both these qualities shine out, it makes a deep impression on us. Their example is a strong incentive for us to build our lives and characters on the same foundation – love and humility. The apostle Paul was conscious of his own leadership influence. He urged the Corinthian Christians to follow him as he followed Christ. We are stunned by his boldness:

Be imitators of me, as I am of Christ (1 Corinthians 11:1, RSV).

The example of Christ

In service

The example of Christ was central to Paul's life and faith. He was keen to know and to have the mind of Christ. He implored others to have that same mind (Philippians 2:2–5). This mind of Christ is characterized by self-giving. In Philippians 2:6–11 Paul was probably quoting from an early Christian hymn which focused on Christ's humiliation and exaltation: he humbled himself by divesting himself of the splendour of deity; he assumed the nature and role of a servant; such is the example of Christ! The hymn clearly refers to the scene in the upper room when the Lord Jesus washed the feet of his disciples (John 13:1–15).

We may marvel at Jesus' humility, but we are not invited to be spectators. Jesus enjoined his disciples, and enjoins us today, to follow his example:

'Now that I, your Lord and Teacher, have washed your feet, you also should wash one another's feet. I have set you an example that you should do as I have done for you' (John 13:14–15).

Our Lord stooped to serve. That should be our posture too, humbling ourselves to minister to others.

In obedience

Second, following Christ's example involves emulating his commitment to his Father's will. ' "My food", said Jesus, "is to do the will of him who sent me and to finish his work" ' (John 4:34; see 6:38). He lived and worked within the orbit of God's purposes. Sometimes God's will produced deep pain and agony. In the Garden of Gethsemane Jesus experienced the trauma of having to drink the bitter cup of suffering. ' "My Father," ' he prayed, ' "if it is possible, may this cup be taken from me. Yet not as I will, but as you will" ' (Matthew 26:39). What a contrast to our waywardness! We love to do our own thing and go our own way. We'll submit to God's will when it suits us. If it involves suffering and sacrifice – no thanks! But Christ has set us the example of one who delights to do the Father's will.

In prayer

Third, we should model our prayer life on that of Jesus. Luke depicts him praying at crucial periods in his ministry. He prayed at his baptism, when he chose to identify himself with sinful men and women (Luke 3:21). He spent a night in prayer before appointing the Twelve (Luke 6:12–13). He prayed before he questioned his disciples as to his true identity (Luke 9:18). He was praying when he was transfigured (Luke 9:29). He assured Simon Peter of his prayer for him, even though he knew that Peter would let him down (Luke 22:32). He struggled in prayer in the Garden of Gethsemane (Luke 22:44). He prayed for his enemies on the cross, and even his final breath was a prayer: ' "Father, into your hands I commit my spirit" ' (Luke 23:46).

No wonder, when Jesus was praying by himself, one of his disciples asked, ' "Lord, teach us to pray" ' (Luke 11:1).

Have we caught this spirit of prayer? Do others catch it from us through seeing us communing daily with God?

In relationships

Fourth, we can learn from the way Jesus related to people. The crowds flocked to hear him because there was something attractive and appealing in his personality. He spoke with authority and sincerity. There was no trace of woolliness or hypocrisy. Jesus was no ascetic: he loved parties, and was even dubbed 'a friend of tax collectors and "sinners" ' (Matthew 11:19; see 9:11). He also paid great attention to children (Mark 10:13–16). And he accepted the love and devotion of Mary – a woman with a rather chequered background. Jesus is our model for relating to others.

In suffering

Finally, he calls us to follow in his footsteps in suffering. He chose to be poor (see 2 Corinthians 8:9); he had no house of his own; he was not even assured of a bed (Luke 9:58). He suffered rejection from his own people (see John 1:11); he was let down by friends, even by his closest followers, but he never held it against them. He suffered an agonizing death on the cross, but instead of cursing he blessed. Years later, the apostle Peter reminded his readers:

> To this you were called, because Christ suffered for you, leaving you an example, that you should follow in his steps. He commited no sin, and no deceit was found in his mouth. When they hurled their insults at him, he did not retaliate; when he suffered, he made no threats. Instead, he entrusted himself to him who judges justly (1 Peter 2:21–23).

As leaders, we must never forget that we are called to suffer. We are followers of the crucified Lord. Christ's attitude and example in service, obedience, prayer, relationships and suffering must be ours as well.

Let us now consider Paul's example in a number of different areas.

The example of Paul

In handling controversial matters (see 1 Corinthians 8)

The Corinthian Christians had written to Paul on the issue of eating food that had been sacrificed to idols. In their city, the meat sold in the market had been ritually offered to Greek gods.

Paul replied, explaining to them that Christians have been given knowledge (verse 1). They acknowledge the existence and supremacy of one God (verses 4–6). Idols have no real existence (verses 4–5), so what can be the harm in eating such food? He gives a fascinating answer. There were probably some new Christians among the Corinthians who had just been freed from serving idols. They wanted to make a clean break. So they refused to eat meat that had been sacrificed to pagan gods. Although all Christians were in fact free to eat such meat, 'stronger' Christians ought to think twice before doing so. They should consider the conscience of their 'weaker' brother. They must never do anything that would harm others (verses 11–13). So here we have the example: Paul himself refused to use his freedom to eat what he pleased. He was sensitive to the welfare of his fellow Christians. What an example for us!

In the difficult issue of freedom and rights (see 1 Corinthians 9)

In chapter 9 Paul goes on to develop the theme of freedom and rights. As an apostle he had every right to be supported by the congregations he had planted. Other apostles travelled with their wives, all expenses paid. Using arguments from everyday working life, the law and the commands of Jesus, Paul showed that he was entitled to total financial support in his apostolic ministry (verses 4–14). But he did not insist on his rights. He wanted to proclaim the gospel in such a way that no-one could accuse him of preaching for money (verse 15). Rather, he was under divine compulsion (verse 16). This gospel had so gripped him (verses 16–18) that he would not allow anything to hinder its proclamation.

Paul was a free man. Politically he was a Roman citizen, not a slave. Spiritually, he enjoyed liberty in Christ. But he deliberately made himself a slave to everyone in order to win them (verse 19). In his approach he identified himself with both Jews and Gentiles, and with those who were weak or deprived (verses 20–22). He was prepared to be 'all things to all men so that by all possible means I might save some' (verse 22).

Paul was a trail-blazer. He shows us the importance of not insisting on our rights, but of using our freedom for the welfare of others. He demonstrated by his example what it means to maintain the priority of proclaiming the gospel. Gripped by the good news, we should be prepared to identify with others and to employ every means to win them for Christ.

In self-discipline

The apostle also enunciated the importance of discipline. He chose the imagery of the racetrack and boxing ring. In the Isthmian Games the athletes would run through the city of Corinth. What was the chief aim of the competitors? – to win the race. So Christians should 'run in such a way as to get the prize' (9:24). This means strict training and running with a goal in view – to breast the tape and win the race (verse 25). Similarly, the boxer would never dream of getting into the ring and beating the air. He would aim his punches at his opponent (verse 26). To be a successful athlete or boxer, you must be the master of your own body (verse 27). So Paul disciplined himself by saying 'no' to fleshly appetites. He controlled and trained his body with regular exercise. Another thing that kept him going was the fear of being disqualified from winning the prize (verse 27b).

His example also challenges us to discipline ourselves. We can't serve God effectively as leaders unless we have first mastered our own bodily appetites.

In pursuing his life's goal

Another passage which is worth careful study is Philippians 3. Here Paul shares his life goals and objectives with his beloved fellow Christians at Philippi.

In verse 17 Paul invites his readers to follow his example in devotion to Christ. For him, the greatest thing in life was to know Christ, to be clothed in his righteousness (verses 8–9), to experience the power of his resurrection and to share in his sufferings (verse 10). Paul prized Jesus Christ above everything else, including his religious pedigree and upbringing as a Jew and Pharisee (verses 5–6). In knowing Christ, the word 'loss' was scribbled across the pages of his past life. The Philippians may have thought Paul rather coarse as the Greek word translated 'loss' literally means 'dung'! Now that Paul had found Christ and was secure in him, his desire was to press on in his Christian race (verses 13–14).

If we take the example of Paul seriously, we will also want to be spiritual pace-setters. Let Christ become the consuming passion of our lives so that we too can say with heartfelt conviction, 'For to me, to live is Christ' (Philippians 1:21).

When Paul exhorted his readers to follow him, he didn't want to make Pauline clones out of them. He wasn't longing to create a host of Paul look-alikes! His deep desire was that we, like him, should make Christ supreme in our lives. Leadership – in terms of setting a good example – should result in personal godliness and in a growing eagerness to please the Lord.

Examples of other New Testament leaders

I suspect that some of you are thinking, 'How on earth can we follow Paul's example? He was an outstanding missionary and apostle. He is in a different league altogether!' How many of us would dare to say, 'Follow me as I follow Paul and as Paul followed Christ'?

Perhaps we can identify more easily with Timothy. He seems to have been a man of nervous temperament, rather timid and cautious. Paul had to remind him that God gives us a spirit of power, love and self-discipline, and not a spirit of timidity (2 Timothy 1:7). When he had to exercise oversight in Ephesus, he must have felt extremely inexperienced and inadequate. Paul, his spiritual father, had to buttress his confidence: 'Don't let anyone look down on you because you are young . . .' (1 Timothy 4:12). Timothy did not enjoy robust health – he was probably afflicted by a stomach complaint. Paul encouraged him to 'use a little wine because of your stomach and your frequent illnesses' (1 Timothy 5:23).

We can readily empathize with Timothy. He presents a picture of an inexperienced leader ministering in a tough situation, handicapped by physical weakness and a nervous temperament. Paul's counsel to Timothy and to us is to remember our commissioning as leaders. Timothy was reminded to 'fan into flame the gift of God, which is in you through the laying on of my hands' (2 Timothy 1:6). This gift empowers (verse 7), and therefore Timothy was to 'be strong in the grace that is in Christ Jesus' (2:1).

In spite of his weaknesses and inadequacies, Timothy was to be a sterling example to the believers in Ephesus:

> Command and teach these things. Don't let anyone look down on you because you are young, but *set an example* . . . in speech, in life, in love, in faith and in purity (1 Timothy 4:11–12, emphasis mine).

Timothy was not to feel inferior because of his age. He was to teach God's Word with authority. At the same time, by his lifestyle and behaviour he should be setting a pattern for godly living, illustrating how a Christian should speak, live, love, exercise faith and pursue holiness.

Example-setting is quite demanding. Timothy had to *devote* himself to 'the public reading of Scripture, to preaching and to teaching' (verse 13); he had to be diligent in every area of service. As he discharged his spiritual oversight, he had to watch his own life and doctrine closely. Paul wrote, 'Persevere in them, because if you do, you will save both yourself and your hearers' (verses 15–16).

Titus was another young member of Paul's missionary task force. He was in charge of the church at Crete. The Christians in Crete were infected by the spirit of the age. There was a tendency to rebel against authority and discipline, and to show very little respect for moral law and order. So Paul encouraged Titus to be self-controlled (Titus 2:6). He pressed Titus to teach sound doctrine and 'in everything set them an example by doing what is good' (verse 7). The teaching of Christian truth and doctrine, accompanied by an exemplary character, was the best way of inculcating true godliness in a licentious age.

Similarly, the apostle Peter appealed to fellow elders to fulfil their God-given responsibilities as shepherds. They were over-seers of God's flock and should be eager to serve. They were not to boss others about or throw their weight around. Instead they were to be *examples* to God's people (1 Peter 5:1–3).

So for the apostles one thing was evident: leaders in the church have an obligation to set an example which will motivate others to godly living and faithful service.

Contemporary and personal examples

At the beginning of this chapter we mentioned that most people learn by copying their peers or gurus. I was amused to read that the disciples of Socrates imitated his stoop long before they followed his philosophy! Just watch a teenager sing his favourite pop songs – it is not difficult to guess which pop star he is imitating. There are peculiar problems in example-setting. In the early sixties I worked with college students in Singapore. It was easy to spot Christian students connected with a certain campus ministry as they spoke English with an American accent. They even held their Bibles and flipped through the pages in a similar fashion to their American mentor. Young Christians tend to imitate their leaders' mannerisms. They may start with the externals but they should not stop there. They should also emulate the things that really matter: a passionate concern for the lost, an appetite for God's Word and a desire for godliness. We should be concerned that they become conformed to the image of Christ (see Romans 12:1–2).

It is interesting that the words used to translate 'example' in Greek are *tupos* and *hupotupōsis*. Both refer to the outline of an artist's sketch. As with all outlines, there is room for us to fill in different colours and details. If we insist on imposing a rigid pattern on everyone's life, we shall overlook God's gifts of creativity and his love of variety.

Personal experience

In August 1984 I was interviewed live on radio in New Zealand. After learning that I had been in active Christian service for twenty-five years, the interviewer asked, 'Who would you say had influenced you most in your leadership style and ministry?'

That's not an easy question to answer, especially when you only have two or three seconds to think! I have since reflected further on her question, and have come up with the following 'answer'.

I am a firm believer in and exponent of expository preaching. Sometimes when I reflect on my own approach, I can detect that I have borrowed so much from two eminent preachers, Dr Martyn Lloyd-Jones and Dr John Stott. As a student in London, I heard them preach regularly for four years. I learned the importance of addressing the whole man from Dr Lloyd-Jones, and the need to build bridges between the world of the Bible and the world of today from John Stott.

My first job was to serve the Chinese church in London as Associate Pastor. Pastor Stephen Wang was the founder-minister of this interdenominational church. He had spent most of his life as headmaster of a large mission school in Beijing, China. When the Communists overran China he was unable to return to his family and teaching responsibilities. The late

Stephen Wang was not the greatest of preachers, neither was he an organizer. But he possessed an amazing quality: his enthusiasm in motivating young people to serve actively in the church.

Pastor Wang also set a good example in not being afraid to bring in abler workers. He reminded me of the well-known American industrialist, Andrew Carnegie. When asked the secret of his company's success, Mr Carnegie said, 'I have a team of smarter men working with me.'

Why is it that I invariably pray with fellow Christians after conversations or interviews? I have been deeply influenced by David Adeney, who was my spiritual mentor. He and I worked together among students in East Asia during the sixties. All who know him are aware of his godly habit of committing every conversation to God in prayer.

At the tender age of thirty-three I assumed responsibilities as General Secretary of IFES! I was thrown into the arena of decision-making that would affect regions and national movements. Looking back, I am so thankful for a chairman who helped me to think biblically and pastorally and who was fully supportive of my ministry. This same man of God in his quiet and informal way stressed the importance of family vacations. I could easily have become a workaholic but he wisely shared with me his own priority of giving time to his wife and growing children. I doubt if I would have learned that lesson by attending formal lectures on the subject but I heeded my chairman's advice because he set such a fine example himself.

I don't want to give the impression that I have learnt only from outstanding preachers and leaders. My life has been enriched through fellowship and working with all kinds of Christians. I have learnt how to be bold and take risks for the Lord Jesus through observing the quiet and steady ministries of staff who labour among students in some of the troubled spots of the world. Although they and their families face danger and harassment for the sake of the gospel, they persist in their service for the Master.

It is quite easy to glamourize front-line workers, but every day when I go to my office I marvel at the team of dedicated workers who steadily and quietly work behind the scenes to back up the staff out on the field. Jacques Beney, for example, was a Swiss banker, but now devotes his energy and skill to the financial operations of our Fellowship. Through his efficient service he sets an example of producing our best for God. I've talked to humble believers in China. They have been through prison because of their faith. They and their families have suffered. Yet I have never been able to detect a single word of bitterness. All I have heard is their gratitude and praise to almighty God for his love and grace. What an example of Christian fortitude! Then, how can I forget a Christian family in England who welcomed me to their home when I was a lonely overseas student? Their love and hospitality stirred me to pray, 'Lord, one day when I have my own home, I am going to invite others in.' God has enabled my wife and me to keep that promise.

What if we fail?

Spiritual leaders are expected in Scripture to set an example in godly living and faithful service. We should pattern our lives and service on Christ and the apostles. Christians learn best from those who exemplify Christian standards. But what if we fail? Can we still exhort others to follow us? Won't they be copying our bad examples?

Our failures can often furnish the setting for learning. But whatever we do, we should never resort to covering up our shortcomings or weaknesses. We must humbly admit them. We must resist any attempt to rationalize our sins, and we should not blame negative circumstances.

Christians find it impossible to pattern their lives on bionic leaders! So we need to be honest and confess our struggles and failures. At the same time, we must demonstrate the reality of God's forgiveness when we repent. Folk will be encouraged when they see God restoring and renewing us. When they fall, they too will know how to turn to God. Thus our example can help them to triumph over defeat.

Chapter Five

THE CHOICE OF LEADERS

The Bible expects sterling qualities in spiritual leaders. After all, we are servants of the most high God. He has called us to represent him as his ambassadors.

Someone may object, 'Where on earth can you find such leaders? – leaders who are prepared to serve God and their contemporaries with humility; leaders who are faithful and trustworthy in their stewardship; leaders who embody the role of shepherds in caring for, feeding and protecting God's people? As for setting godly examples, just name me a few who qualify!'

Now we have to admit that there are no perfect leaders. The chapter entitled 'Leaders are human too!' (chapter 13) will dispel the myth of the infallible leader (see also chapter 14). But it is tempting for us to lower biblical standards and it is easy to appoint unsuitable candidates to fill leadership vacancies, especially when time is short.

Some years ago, at a famous Eisteddfod (music festival) in Wales, a competing choir committed a musical blunder. They pitched the first note of their piece too low. The pianist, realizing their mistake, transposed the music to a lower key, so the voices and the accompaniment blended harmoniously. The audience received the performance with loud applause. However, the chief adjudicator stood up and marched over to the piano. Without a word, he struck the correct pitch. Then he sat down again. Choir, pianist and audience got the message!

We must resist the temptation to tamper with biblical expectations and standards, but we must realize that leaders do not mature overnight. No-one can claim to be one hundred per cent fitted to his job from the start. There is room for growth. We should therefore fix our eyes on Christians who are growing disciples and open to God.

How then are we to choose our leaders? What are some biblical guidelines to help us know the type of people we should be appointing? Let's look first at the Old Testament.

Leaders in the Old Testament

The nation of Israel was a theocracy. This meant that God was the supreme leader and king. Subsequently all leaders – monarchs, prophets and priests – operated under God's authority. They represented him and never possessed absolute authority like the neighbouring pagan priest-kings. The leaders of Israel were always accountable to God.

Now it is true that kingship was hereditary in the united monarchy of Israel and the southern kingdom of Judah. Nevertheless, the writer of the books of Chronicles invariably judges the performance of each king by his fidelity or infidelity to Yahweh, especially in respect of keeping the law (see 2 Chronicles 14:2–6; 17:3–6; 20:31–33; 25:25–28; 33:21–24). God expected high moral and spiritual qualities of those who sat on David's throne.

The tribe of Levi produced men who served as priests and Levites. The priests traced their ancestry back to Aaron, the brother of Moses. They performed various rituals, including the statutory sacrifices, and they conducted the worship in the tabernacle and the temple. They were ably assisted by the Levites. Both groups were responsible for instructing God's people in the law. As religious leaders they had prescribed duties and a code to follow. The prophets were unique. They were God's spokesmen. They declared his Word with authority. 'Thus says the Lord' is a familiar formula which carries tremendous authority.

The qualities expected of prophets correspond closely to those required of leaders in the New Testament. There was no automatic dynastic succession of prophets. Genuine leaders are personally commissioned by God. Let's briefly examine the major qualifications of a prophet or a spiritual leader.

1 The leader has a deep experience of God

Let's consider two outstanding Old Testament leaders, Moses and Isaiah. At the foot of Mount Horeb God addressed Moses by name (Exodus 3:4). He then personally commissioned him as Israel's deliverer (verses 7–10). Moses was reluctant to assume this onerous responsibility (see 3:11; 4:1, 10, 13). He even pleaded with God to appoint someone else! But God promised to stand by Moses as he tried to fulfil his awesome task (3:12; 4:12). It was because of his relationship with the Lord that Moses was able to confront powerful Pharaoh and lead the people of Israel out of slavery. Throughout the wilderness wandering he met constantly with God. At one of their summit meetings the Law was given. In one inspiring encounter, Moses boldly asked the Lord to show him his glory (Exodus 33:18). Only a man who had a deep experience of God could make such an amazing request.

The prophet Isaiah had a breathtaking encounter with the sovereign Lord. He had been a recognized religious leader in the court of King Uzziah, who had died after a long reign. Isaiah was in the temple, probably feeling rather despondent, when he was suddenly given a magnificent vision of God (see Isaiah 6).

First he saw God sitting upon his throne. The throne of Judah was empty, but the throne of heaven is always occupied. He caught a glimpse of God's holiness and glory. Then he heard the song of the seraphim:

> 'Holy, holy, holy is the LORD
>   Almighty;
>   the whole earth is full of his
>   glory' (verse 3).

Both Moses and Isaiah were given a deep, intimate experience of God. In each case this formed the basis of their calling as God's chosen leaders.

2 The leader has a growing awareness of his sin and inadequacy

Whenever we come face to face with the Lord God, we become more aware of our own creatureliness and inadequacy. In the blazing light of his holiness, we are deeply conscious of our sins. The hymn-writer has aptly expressed this fact:

And they who fain would serve Thee best
Are conscious most of wrong within.

Isaiah experienced this. In chapter 5 he had pronounced six 'woes' or curses against drunkards, exploiters, liars and evil-doers (verses 8, 11, 18, 20–22). But as he records in chapter 6, when he contemplated the absolute purity of God he pronounced the seventh woe on himself. 'Woe to me!' he cried out. He confessed that he and his people were polluted and contaminated by sin.

Confession was immediately followed by cleansing and forgiveness. The prophet's lips were cleansed by a burning coal taken from the altar (Isaiah 6:6–7). The altar was where sacrifices were performed. It usually reeked of blood. So it is a reminder that without the shedding of blood there is no forgiveness of sin (Hebrews 9:22).

No leader can ever come to God with an air of arrogance. None of us can say, 'God, I'm your man. Look at my academic degrees and achievements. Just trace my spiritual pedigree – it's pretty impressive. And as for my gifts and experience . . .'.

God has no room for proud leaders. He calls those who prostrate themselves before him. They are the ones who recognize the gravity of sin and God's grace in forgiving them. Moses, Isaiah, Jeremiah, Ezekiel, Daniel, Peter, John, Paul – all these spiritual giants had to humble themselves in the presence of the mighty Lord.

When I interview potential staff, I'm rather wary of those who boast of their gifts and experience. They give the impression that they're doing God a favour by sacrificing their promising careers to join IFES. I sometimes wish I had the guts to rebuke them! But the men and women who serve

God best are those who are conscious of their failings and inadequacies. They dare to respond only because the Lord has called, forgiven and empowered them.

3 The leader has a deep sense of God's call

After Isaiah's guilt had been removed, he heard God's call. ' "Whom shall I send? And who will go for us?" ' (Isaiah 6:8). The sovereign and holy Lord had a special assignment. He did not force Isaiah to enlist. But having received God's pardon, Isaiah responded immediately: ' "Here am I. Send me!" ' Note his enthusiastic obedience – 'I'm available, I'm prepared to serve you!' Too often when God calls, we excuse ourselves, 'Lord, send someone else!'

Some leaders are called to assume extremely difficult and dangerous responsibilities. Take Jeremiah for instance. Poor Jeremiah! He was commissioned to serve God at one of the most critical epochs in Judah's history – 627–586 BC.

God in his sovereign purpose was going to hand his people over to the Babylonians. He was going to chastise his people through painful exile. As expected, the political and religious rulers turned against Jeremiah. He was branded a traitor when in fact he was a true patriot. His fellow prophets and priests bullied him too. The final blow came when Pashhur, a priest who was also the chief officer of the temple, had Jeremiah flogged and his legs put in the stocks.

Jeremiah could no longer bottle up his emotions. He unleashed his feelings at God. Surely a prophet should be entitled to some respect!

> O LORD, you deceived me, and
>   I was deceived;
>   you overpowered me and
>   prevailed.
> I am ridiculed all day long;
>   everyone mocks me.
> Whenever I speak, I cry out
>   proclaiming violence and
>   destruction.

> So the word of the LORD has
>   brought me
>   insult and reproach all day
>   long.
> But if I say, 'I will not
>   mention him
>   or speak any more in his
>   name,'
> his word is in my heart like a
>   burning fire,
>   shut up in my bones.
> I am weary of holding it in;
>   indeed, I cannot (Jeremiah 20:7–9).

He might have resigned and given up his prophetic office. He might have retired to a quiet life. But he simply couldn't. Why not? Because 'his word is in my heart like a burning fire, shut up in my bones'.

God's message is fire. You can't keep fire inside you! You have to spread God's word. There's no other way.

Jeremiah never forgot that God had called and appointed him for a special mission. Mocked, ridiculed and at times burdened with self-doubt, this man of God weathered the storms because he knew that God had called him to fulfil his purpose.

The serving seven

A crisis had erupted in the Jerusalem church. Amidst great growth (the number of disciples was increasing – see Acts 6:1) an organizational problem had surfaced. It might have resulted in an ugly rift because it affected two communities – the Greek-speaking and Aramaic-speaking believers. Problem? Somehow the Greek-speaking widows were being overlooked in the distribution of food.

The Twelve became involved and summoned the assembly. The apostles maintained that their main priority was the ministry of the Word and prayer (verses 2, 4), but suggested that this administrative problem could be solved by appointing seven officers. Church members were pleased with this solution and seven men were chosen and presented to the apostles.

Although the seven were appointed for routine and administrative chores, they had to be 'full of the Spirit and wisdom' (verse 3). The apostles did not recommend that the church should look for capable managers. Character came first. Leadership in God's church has to be undertaken by Spirit-filled men – men directed by the Holy Spirit. Such people put Christ above all things, for the Spirit always exalts Christ (see John 16:14). The second quality required was that of wisdom. The seven had to be wise administrators. They needed organizational abilities and wisdom to know how to handle sensitive situations.

Thus two prerequisites were expected of God's servants in the early church – Spirit-filled characters and wisdom to accomplish their task.

The selection of spiritual overseers

The apostle Paul laid down stringent requirements for the appointment of leaders. Titus was exhorted to appoint elders (note the plural) for the congregations in Crete (Titus 1:5).

Most scholars are agreed that the offices of elders (*presbuteroi*) and bishops (or overseers – *episkopoi*) are interchangeable. Titus 1:6–7 reinforces this fact. Some consider that the term 'elder' is a reference to their *status*. The word *presbuteros* is used of an older man (1 Timothy 5:1). The elders directed the affairs of the church, and some were engaged in the work of preaching and teaching. These were 'worthy of double honour' – they should have received a double stipend (1 Timothy 5:17)!

Terms like 'bishop' or 'overseer' describe ministry *function*. As we focus our attention on the qualities and responsibilities of elders or overseers (1 Timothy 3:1–7), we need to stress that the apostle was thinking of *mature* leaders. He warned Timothy against appointing new converts or novices (1 Timothy 3:6). The modern equivalents of these leaders include ministers of churches, recognized lay leaders, missionaries and those who have spiritual oversight in Christian organizations and agencies.

When a youth fellowship in a church or a college Christian fellowship is selecting its leaders, it would be unrealistic to apply the qualities expected of fairly mature leaders. For them, the basic requirements in Acts 6 should be sufficient. Young leaders ought to be committed Christians with leadership gifts to match their responsibilities.

Let's turn our attention to the qualities we should look for in appointing leaders for God's church. Below you will find a table which compares the qualities listed in 1 Timothy 3 with those in Titus 1.

1 Timothy 3	Titus 1
Personal character	*Personal character*
Above reproach (2)	Blameless (6)
Temperate (2)	Disciplined (8)
Self-controlled (2)	Self-controlled (8)
Not given to much wine (3)	Not given to much wine (7)
Not quarrelsome (3)	Not overbearing, not violent (7)
Not lover of money (3)	Not pursuing dishonest gain (7)
Respectable (2)	Upright (8)
Gentle (3)	Loves what is good (8)
Good reputation with outsiders (7)	Holy (8)
Leadership functions	*Leadership functions*
Hospitable (2)	Hospitable (8)
Able to teach others (2)	Hold firmly to the message, encourage sound doctrine and refute critics (9)
Family relationships	*Family relationships*
Husband of one wife (2)	Husband of one wife (6)
Good management of family with respectful and obedient children (4–5)	Believing and obedient children (6)
Warning	
Not a recent convert (6)	

First, we note the emphasis on character. Leaders are not chosen because they are intelligent, powerful and rich. Some churches make the mistake of appointing senior members who are pillars of society and carry clout. Unless they are full of the Holy Spirit and possess Christlike characters, they will import and impart carnal values to their churches or Christian organizations.

We note the stress on leaders being self-controlled and temperate (reflecting the fruit of the Spirit, see Galatians 5:22–23). Their lives are to be marked by holiness. Leaders should also have a good standing in their community. The world loves to attack Christian leaders. Whenever a pastor or Sunday school teacher commits a moral offence, it hits the headlines in the popular tabloids. High moral standards are expected of those who hold office in God's church. Therefore those who exercise leadership in the church should be men and women of the utmost moral integrity.

Spiritual leaders are required to be hospitable. The Greek word literally means 'a lover of strangers'. In Paul's day, there were many itinerant prophets and evangelists. These men required board and lodging. The inns of the first century were notorious dens of iniquity. The leaders should willingly open their homes to these servants of the Lord.

Through practising hospitality, Christian leaders are able to get to know their church members and also newcomers. Moreover, it is a good practical expression of love and care for those who are lonely and in need of friendship.

Spiritual leaders are expected to be teachers who communicate Christian truth. This does not necessarily mean that they should all be preachers. But they must be able to hold firm to God's Word, using it to build up others in their faith and to expose false teaching.

The family relationships of leaders should also come under careful consideration. This is all the more important in an age of increasing marital and family breakdowns. An overseer should have only one wife. The early church upheld the monogamous pattern of marriage. It is important that only those who maintain marital fidelity should be leaders in the church.

Since leaders have to set an example, good family relationships are important. According to Paul, their children should be believers and should show them respect.

There is heated discussion amongst Christians as to the application of this standard. What of the children of recognized church leaders or missionaries who do not profess faith in Christ? Should these leaders resign from their positions? Besides, can any leader guarantee the salvation of his children?

These are valid questions and should be answered sympathetically. However, we should expect leaders to set an example in their homes. Even if their children are not committed Christians, they should be considerate and well-mannered (see 1 Timothy 3:4–5). And leaders who are parents should earnestly pray and work for the conversion of their offspring. The argument in the Pastoral Epistles is simply this: the Christian family is a microcosm of the church. The overseer who exercises his headship in his family will be in a better position to preside over the affairs of God's household. There is no greater testimony than a Christian leader serving the Lord with the enthusiastic participation of his family. Like Joshua he can declare:

'As for me and my household, we will serve the LORD' (Joshua 24:15).

Let's heed Paul's warning against the appointing of a recent convert to a position of leadership. The Greek word *neophutos*, from which we get our English word 'neophyte', means 'newly planted'. Young converts are like newly planted trees. They need time to strike roots and grow.

When Paul gave Timothy instructions about the appointment of deacons, he firmly insisted:

They must first be tested; and then if there is nothing against them, let them serve as deacons (1 Timothy 3:10).

Deacons are also servants of the church. They were first appointed to look after administrative matters. But like elders or overseers, they were to possess sound characters and to impart sound teaching (verses 8–9).

The word translated 'test' is the Greek *dokimazō*. It was a

68

word used to describe the examination of lambs that were to be offered for sacrifice. These animals had to be without blemish. It was also used for the selection and appointment of senators. They had to undergo careful scrutiny before they could hold high office in the Roman Senate. Today we need to select our leaders with prayer and care. Only proven and faithful servants of Jesus Christ should be appointed.

Leadership appointment procedures

It's always best for the leadership team to initiate the search for new leaders. Responsible leaders can then consider prayerfully names of potential leaders.

We need to recognize those whom the Spirit has appointed as overseers and shepherds of God's church (see Acts 20:28). They should be Christians who sense that God has personally called them to service in his kingdom. They should also be made aware of the qualities the Bible requires of spiritual leaders.

One or two members of the leadership team should then meet with the candidates. Job responsibilities should be clearly spelled out. It's important that the potential leaders know what is expected of them. They must be willing to give high priority to their leadership responsibilities. This means scheduling time for their assignments.

If the potential leaders are married, their partners should be consulted. It's essential that they have the support of their family.

Leaders need public recognition and affirmation. When a leader is prepared to serve in accordance with the terms outlined, the appointment should be made known to the entire membership. He should then be publicly commissioned. When Joshua was appointed the new leader of Israel, Moses and Eleazar the priest commissioned him in the presence of the entire assembly (Numbers 27:18–23). Similarly, when the seven administrators were chosen, the apostles publicly laid hands on them and presented them to the entire congregation (Acts 6:6).

Such public commissioning serves two valuable functions. First, it strengthens the call and the convictions of the leaders.

In the face of discouragement, they can look back to this memorable event. They will be reminded of their solemn vows to serve God and his people. They will also remember that it was God who called and equipped them for service. When he calls, he enables.

Second, at a public commissioning members of the church or fellowship participate in their leaders' consecration. They acknowledge that God has set apart these men and women for special leadership responsibilities. They pledge to support and pray for them. Thus a new bond of partnership is forged.

Chapter Six

JESUS THE MASTER TRAINER

Training new workers is an integral part of our ministry as spiritual leaders. How do we train a new generation of leaders? What are our biblical goals in forming leaders? What can we glean from Christ's strategy and efforts in training the Twelve?

Before we answer these questions we have to deal with a preliminary objection: *can* we *train* spiritual leaders? Some Christians are wary of the term 'training'. They subscribe to the view that you can train dogs or monkeys to perform, but you can't train people to be godly leaders. Exponents of this theory equate training with the imparting of skills and techniques. Trainees simply acquire the tricks of the trade. Such folk are critical (and rightly so) of certain evangelists who naïvely announce that they have devised a foolproof formula for evangelism. They claim that if Christians attend their courses, buy their manuals and use their booklets, they will become first-rate witnesses and clock up many decisions for Christ.

In some countries, special Christian leadership conferences and seminars are offered to the Christian public. Leaders or potential leaders spend a week-end undergoing intensive training so as to improve their leadership skills. They are awarded diplomas and return to their congregations priding themselves on their new insights. They are going to change things. Give them a free hand and they will guarantee growth.

Both sets of trainees soon discover that witnesses and leaders are not produced overnight. Training conferences, though helpful, have limited value. Moreover, no single way of presenting the gospel guarantees a response. We have to start where our enquirers are: we need to be sensitive to the questions they are asking and help them to move from a position of no faith to one of faith in the living Christ. Church structures and individual Christians have inbuilt complexities. Agents of change need to be trusted and respected, and all this inevitably takes time. So any form of training that offers simple formulae or instant success should be treated with deep suspicion.

My colleagues in Latin America have substituted the word *formacion* for the word 'training'. *Formacion* is a Spanish word used of the forming and shaping of character. They maintain that the New Testament lays stress on the character development of leaders rather than on the acquisition of particular management skills. Whilst there is much to commend this emphasis, we need not eliminate the word 'training' from our vocabulary. It occurs in some Bible texts, for example Matthew 13:52, 1 Timothy 4:7 and 2 Timothy 3:16. When we speak of training in this book, we include both character formation and the imparting of specific service skills.

Jesus the master trainer

No study on the theme of spiritual leadership is ever complete without a careful examination of how Jesus trained the Twelve. In 1871 Professor A. B. Bruce of Glasgow published his classic volume entitled *The Training of the Twelve*. This 552–page book contains a gold-mine of material relating to the content, principles and methods of our Lord's training of the Twelve. It is rewarding to wade through this comprehensive textbook on leadership training.

Dr Robert E. Coleman, formerly Professor of Evangelism and Missions at Ashbury, has written a book called *The Master Plan of Evangelism*. Published in 1963, it is a more contemporary treatment of the subject studied by Professor Bruce a century earlier. Dr Coleman invites his readers to consider the strategy and priorities of Jesus. He had three short years of public ministry. During this brief period, the Saviour concentrated his time and energy on training the Twelve for world conquest. Jesus' tactics are classified under the following chapter headings: 'Selection'; 'Association'; 'Consecration';

'Impartation'; 'Demonstration'; 'Delegation'; 'Supervision'; 'Reproduction'. Each of these themes is substantiated by material from the four gospels. Every section ends with contemporary applications.

We do well to watch the master trainer at work. In a day when there are immense spiritual needs and a dearth of high-calibre Christian leaders, there is a pressing need to reassess our training philosophy and methodology. We shall look briefly at the biblical data and then seek to apply the abiding lessons for the equipping of spiritual leaders.

1 He called and chose them

'Follow me': with these two words the Lord Jesus summoned Peter, James and John to be his disciples (Matthew 4:19). Levi the tax collector also responded to a similar command (Luke 5:27). The Twelve did not volunteer for special service: Jesus called them individually; he took the initiative.

Our Lord hand-picked his disciples; he did not select them at random. We know that he spent considerable time watching and getting to know them before he chose them and designated them to be apostles. The selection of the apostolic band was of the utmost importance to Jesus' mission. He called them after spending all night in prayer (Luke 6:12–16).

A quick glance at the Twelve indicates that they were a mixed bunch! Simon Peter was swift and impulsive and was the spokesman of the group. Thomas, by contrast, was rather cautious and given to doubts. The Zebedee brothers, James and John, like Peter and Andrew, were fishermen by trade. They had a telling nickname: 'Sons of Thunder'! Hot-tempered characters are not the easiest people to live and work with! Philip seems to have been the curious one, always asking questions. Matthew and Simon the Zealot were at opposite political poles. As a tax collector, Matthew was dubbed by the Jews 'a running dog and a traitor'; Simon the Zealot on the other hand was a hot-headed nationalist. Had Jesus not called them both to follow him, Simon would probably have plunged a sword right through Matthew's heart! We don't know much about Bartholomew or Judas the son of James – perhaps they were fairly ordinary characters. However, we are familiar with Judas Iscariot, the traitor.

In many ways they were a motley crew. So why were they chosen? Jesus singled them out, not because they were brilliant, powerful or wealthy, but because of their capacity to learn. Christ spotted potential in them. We detect this in a brief conversation between him and Simon Peter. Bishop John V. Taylor offers this insight:

> To say 'You are Simon: you shall be called Peter' ['*rock-like*'] is to make a man responsible for the contrast between what is and what should be. To hold a man responsible means both an act of judgment and an act of faith (Taylor 1972:97).

Lessons for today

How do we recruit our leaders? Do we wait for gifted personalities to turn up and volunteer their services? That's not Jesus' method. Like him, we need to take the initiative in spotting and recruiting workers. We probably won't find ready-made quality leaders. So we need to assess people's potential. Are they growing disciples, hungering after God and willing to follow him wholeheartedly? Are they open to be taught and equipped as servant-leaders?

Where possible, let's aim at picking a *team* which reflects different backgrounds and gifts rather than a bunch of gifted individuals.

To do this effectively we must be amongst the people so that we can single out potential workers. There's no foolproof system in choosing leaders. Some may let us down: Judas turned out to be a bad apple. There are risks in any selection process.

2 He spent time with them

Mark expressly records:

> He appointed twelve – designating them apostles – that they might be with him and that he might send them out to preach (Mark 3:14).

This was a deliberate policy of Jesus. He wanted his disciples to be with him so they lived, travelled and worked together. Their spiritual equipping was his primary concern.

But someone may object, 'What about the needs of the crowds? By concentrating on the Twelve, wasn't Jesus guilty of favouritism or elitism?'

As we read through the gospel accounts, we observe that he did not neglect the crowds. He taught them and fed them. He healed large numbers of sick people and cast out demons. He also had time to relate to individuals. Just think of Nicodemus, the woman at the well, Zacchaeus, blind Bartimaeus the beggar, Mary, Martha, Lazarus and the Syro-Phoenician woman. But although crowds and individuals dogged his footsteps, Jesus made sure that he always spent time with his disciples.

Coleman writes:

Frequently He would take them with Him in a retreat to some mountainous area of the country where He was relatively unknown, seeking to avoid publicity as far as possible. They took trips together to Tyre and Sidon to the Northwest (Mark 7:24; Matt. 15:21); to the 'borders of Decapolis' (Mark 7:31; cf., Matt. 15:29) and 'the parts of Dalmanutha' to the Southeast of Galilee (Mark 8:10; cf., Matt. 15:39); and to the 'villages of Caesarea Philippi' to the Northeast (Mark 8:27; cf., Matt. 16:13). These journeys were made partly because of the opposition of the Pharisees and the hostility of Herod, but primarily because Jesus felt the need to get alone with His disciples. Later He spent several months with His disciples in Perea east of the Jordan (Luke 13:22–19:28; John 10:40–11:54; Matt. 19:1–20:34; Mark 10:1–52). As opposition mounted there, Jesus 'walked no more openly among the Jews, but departed thence into the country near to the wilderness, into a city called Ephraim; and there He tarried with His disciples' (John 11:54). When at last the time came for Him to go to Jerusalem, He significantly 'took the twelve disciples apart' from the rest as He made His way slowly to the city (Matt. 20:17; cf., Mark 10:32).

In view of this, it is not surprising that during passion week Jesus scarcely ever let His disciples out of His sight (Coleman 1963:41).

For three years, the lives of the Twelve and the Master were intertwined. He was among them, always available to answer their questions and meet their needs. True, there were many demands on his time, but he chose to live transparently before them.

Coleman concludes:

And so it was. The time which Jesus invested in these few disciples was so much more by comparison to that given to others that it can only be regarded as a deliberate strategy. He actually spent more time with His disciples than with everybody else in the world put together (Coleman 1963:42–43).

Lessons for today

We can't produce instant leaders just as we make instant coffee and instant noodles! We must be prepared to invest time and resources in the people whom we seek to train. How easy it is for us to respond to all kinds of different needs and overlook the priority of training our new workers. Our 'democratic' structures and ethos insist that leaders should be available at all times. So we become need-meeters and problem-solvers rather than trainers or disciple-makers.

Dr Christopher Chavasse, former Bishop of Rochester, once said that if he had his ministry over again, he would 'work amongst the few, and give them back to the many' (quoted by Eddison 1984:22). How wise! It is only in the multiplying of workers that we can meet the increasing needs and share the burdens of God's people.

3 He taught them

Jesus could have groomed his future kingdom-builders by getting them to appreciate the uniqueness of their relationship with him and experience of him. After all, what greater privilege than to be intimately associated with the Son of God and to watch him perform his miracles at first hand?

But spiritual experience, though valuable, was not to be their foundation. Jesus assumed the role of teacher and, as the title 'disciple' implies, the Twelve were his students. His school didn't have set time-tables. The disciples didn't turn up for regular lectures. Their classroom was the world around them and their teacher was always on the move. They learnt many mind-boggling and eternal truths from the master teacher.

Just reflect on the *content* of his teaching. As we study his famous sermon on the mount (Matthew 5–7), which was first delivered primarily for the benefit of the Twelve, we can almost hear Jesus introducing them to membership, priorities and lifestyle in God's kingdom. He taught them how he came to fulfil the Law and to give it a deeper meaning. Keeping the Law meant more than obeying the letter of its text. It involved a new righteousness, following God's way of handling issues like murder, adultery, divorce, oath-taking, personal revenge and relating to our enemies (Matthew 5:17ff.).

As teacher, he instructed them on the nature and practice of true spirituality (Matthew 6:1–18). They had to adopt a 'first things first' attitude to life: seeking God's kingdom and trusting God were the best antidotes to anxiety. Jesus challenged his followers to be discerning and to make the right choices: to enter the narrow gate (7:13–14), to build on firm foundations and to do his will (7:24–27). He offered profound teaching on prayer and also gave them *the* model prayer (7:7–12; 6:9–13).

All four gospels preserve the dialogues and arguments which Jesus had with the Jews. The Twelve watched him debating with the religious authorities and gained valuable insight into how they should interpret and apply the Old Testament teaching on controversial topics such as sabbath-keeping, traditions of the elders, citizenship responsibilities, divorce and marriage and the life to come (*e.g.* Matthew 19:1–12; 22:15–33; Mark 2:23–27).

A large chunk of the fourth gospel is devoted to Jesus' final discourse (John 13–16). He revealed precious truths about himself, the Holy Spirit, spiritual fruitfulness, the importance of loving one another, expectant prayer and facing trials and persecutions.

The synoptic gospels contain numerous parables (*e.g.* Matthew 13; Luke 15–16). These delightful stories were not only entertaining; they were also didactic in thrust. The hearers – both the crowds and the disciples – were forced to think through their powerful lessons. Jesus often had to provide the key to their underlying meaning. Once he paused to ask his pupils, ' "Have you understood all these things?" ' (Matthew 13:51).

Jesus patiently explained his mission to the Twelve, and the gospel writers devote considerable space to his death and resurrection (Matthew 21–28; Mark 11–16; Luke 19–24; John 12–21). Even after his resurrection Jesus was giving the disciples final instructions.

Christ's teaching left an indelible impression on his disciples. They must have committed to memory much of his instruction. But as we considered earlier, he made his disciples think through real-life issues and problems; he didn't stuff their heads with facts. Neither did he infuse into them abstract theology and philosophy. When he wanted to warn his followers against the legalism and fallacies of the Pharisees, he didn't organize Course 105, 'The Philosophy and Theology of Pharisaism'! He exposed them to the cut and thrust of his debates with these religious hypocrites.

Paulo Freire, a well-known Brazilian educationalist, contrasts two types of education. First there is 'narrative education', thus called because the teachers are *narrating subjects* and the students, *listening objects*. In this educational process students are simply containers; their teachers deposit knowledge and information in them. Freire dubs this the 'banking' concept of education.

The second method of education, which Freire strongly advocates, is to do with problem-posing. The teacher and students together confront reality and help each other to work through the issues with a critical mind. Freire writes, 'Whereas banking education anaesthetizes and inhibits creative power, problem-posing education involves a constant unveiling of reality' (quoted by Stott 1982:175).

Jesus used both the narrative and problem-posing methods in teaching his disciples. Before his ascension, he charged the Eleven to make disciples and teach them ' "to obey everything I have commanded you . . . " ' (Matthew 28:20). The infant church faithfully devoted themselves to the apostles' teaching (Acts 2:42). The disciples emulated the example of their master teacher.

Lessons for today

Leaders are expected to communicate spiritual truth. Whether we teach a large congregation or a tiny group, we need to understand what we are teaching. We must have a firm grasp of Scripture and basic doctrine, otherwise we shall not be in a position to build up others in their faith.

Christ's emphasis on teaching should also be ours. Well-taught leaders will think biblically and this is a crucial base from which to communicate truth to others.

We need to review our teacher-training programme. What priority do we give to systematic teaching? Are leaders provided with opportunities and incentives to improve their teaching skills?

Good teaching relates to life. The lecture-room approach to Christian education has its limitations. As Freire has cautioned us, we must not simply deposit facts in our trainees; we need to get them to work through problems. The more 'live' situations we expose our leaders to, the better their training.

4 He revealed himself to them

Our Lord did not begin his ministry by openly declaring his deity and Messiahship to his disciples. That would simply have dazzled and overwhelmed them. He chose to reveal his identity and his mission in stages; it was a gradual process.

John the Baptist stirred up the curiosity of Andrew and another disciple by referring to Jesus as 'the Lamb of God' (John 1:36). These two disciples struck up a conversation with Jesus and asked where he was staying. He replied, 'Come, and you will see' (verse 39). They spent that day with him.

At the beginning, Jesus' disciples made some tentative

guesses as to his identity. Andrew thought he was the Messiah (verse 41), and Philip, the prophet that Moses had pointed to (verse 45); Nathaniel confessed him as the Son of God, the King of Israel (verse 49). But Jesus simply referred to himself as 'the Son of Man' (verse 51).

As the disciples listened to his teaching, they realized that he was very different from the rabbinic teachers. These men always quoted a multitude of authorities and scholars, but Jesus used the formula, 'Amen, Amen', which has been variously translated, 'Verily, verily' (KJV), 'Truly, truly' (RSV) and 'I tell you the truth' (NIV).

As the disciples watched him heal the sick, cure those suffering from leprosy, give sight to the blind and make whole the crippled, they recognized that these were signs. These signposts focused attention on Jesus' messianic powers and characteristics (Luke 4:18–21).

While in prison, John the Baptist began to doubt whether Jesus was truly the Messiah. He sent his disciples to check out Christ's credentials. Jesus' reply was most revealing:

'Go back and report to John what you hear and see: The blind receive sight, the lame walk, those who have leprosy are cured, the deaf hear, the dead are raised, and the good news is preached to the poor' (Matthew 11:4–5).

For Jesus' own disciples, this was evidence enough to convince them that their Lord was someone unique. How could they remain unchanged when they kept company with one who could calm storms, walk on water, multiply loaves and fishes to feed vast multitudes?

Towards the end of his public ministry, at Caesarea Philippi, Jesus began to ask his disciples probing questions. Gossip about his identity was already rife, so to start the ball rolling he asked who the crowds were saying he was. He received a host of answers: a prophet, John the Baptist, Elijah, Jeremiah (Matthew 16:14)! Then, looking straight at his disciples, he asked them who they thought he was. Peter answered, ' "You are the Christ, the Son of the living God" ' (verse 16). In response, Jesus commended Peter for his confession, declaring that it did not stem from human understanding but was revealed to him from above (verse 17). It was only then that Jesus began to explain his mission to his disciples. He had come to suffer, to die and to be raised to life (verse 21). His disciples too had to deny themselves and take up their crosses and follow him (verse 24). If Christ had unfolded his mission and called for such sacrifice at the outset, he would probably not have had any disciples at all!

From that critical point on, Jesus began to unveil more of himself to them. The inner circle of Peter, James and John watched him being transfigured before them and heard the voice of the Father declaring, ' "This is my Son, whom I love; with him I am well pleased. Listen to him!" ' (Matthew 17:1–8). Jesus commanded them to keep under wraps all that they had witnessed until after the resurrection.

In the upper room, Jesus left them in no doubt as to who he really was. To Thomas's enquiry as to where he was going, Jesus replied, ' "I am the way and the truth and the life. No-one comes to the Father except through me" ' (John 14:6). Philip, not fully understanding this statement, requested, ' "Lord, show us the Father and that will be enough for us" ' (verse 8). We can almost detect a sigh in Jesus' answer: ' "Don't you know me, Philip, even after I have been among you such a long time? Anyone who has seen me has seen the Father" ' (verse 9). Here, Jesus is claiming to mirror God.

But the most remarkable disclosure of all was the promise of the Holy Spirit. He is the *paraklētos* – one who would stand alongside them. As counsellor he would guide them into all truth and remind them of all that Jesus had been teaching them (John 14:26; 16:13).

In Luke's preface to the book of Acts he describes the post-resurrection ministry of Jesus:

> . . . he showed himself to these men and gave many convincing proofs that he was alive. He appeared to them over a period of forty days and spoke about the kingdom of God (Acts 1:3).

The risen Christ went on reassuring them of his victory over death. He continued to reveal to them God's plan for his new kingdom and the role they would be called upon to play in it.

Lessons for today

Sometimes we drown young leaders with a flood of facts and figures, not to mention responsibilities. They will inevitably feel overwhelmed; they can't see how the various bits and pieces fit into the whole.

In our training of new leaders we need to help them discover God's plan for their lives and work in stages. Confidence in him is built up gradually. It will be marvellous to hear them testify after they've exercised their leadership gifts, 'What a mighty God we serve! He gives us strength to cope with our tasks and wisdom to handle problems!'

If we are grooming leaders to take over our jobs, we should first orientate them, then gradually share with them the joys, opportunities and struggles which leadership entails. They will certainly appreciate such 'revelations'.

5 He assigned them practical tasks

Christ gave practical assignments to his disciples. He delegated the task of seating the five thousand in orderly groups (Mark 6:39), and when the meal was over the disciples had to take charge of the clearing-up operation (verse 43).

After months of being with Jesus and watching him teaching, healing and casting out demons, they were sent on a restricted mission. In Matthew 10, Jesus gathered the Twelve together and gave them authority to heal, to exorcize evil spirits and to announce the coming of his kingdom.

He issued them with clear directions for their mission. For a start, they were to restrict their ministry to the Jews, 'the lost sheep of Israel' (verses 5–6). Since they were on a short-term field trip, they were to travel light (verses 9–10). Their journey ahead would be dangerous because they were being sent out like sheep among wolves (verse 16). There was the likelihood of opposition (verses 17–18), but the Spirit of God would stand by them, enabling them to testify with boldness and wisdom (verses 19–20). When they entered a town or village, they were to look for people who would welcome them and who responded to their message (verses 11–13). They were not to be surprised if some rejected them (verses 13–15).

So they tackled this assignment. Mark tells us that they went out two by two (Mark 6:7), a wise strategy as leaders need companionship and support.

Lessons for today

Training is one-sided if it only consists of theory. Of course we should impart knowledge through lectures and seminars. Leaders should be encouraged to study relevant texts and books. But practical service *must* be integrated into our leadership training programme. People learn best through on-the-job training! This is the approach of Jesus the master trainer.

We shall be wise if, like him, we begin with 'controlled' experiments. It can be suicidal to send a preacher-in-training out to deliver his first sermon before a large congregation! He could first gain considerable experience and confidence by speaking to a Christian youth group, for example.

Sometimes, because of crying needs and a shortage of experienced leaders, we throw young workers in at the deep end. Remarkably, some have survived, but a good number have floundered. Just as Jesus gave clear directives, we too need to ensure that new workers are given sufficient orientation and clear instructions so that they can successfully accomplish their tasks.

6 He evaluated their work

After the Twelve had completed their mission (Mark 6:12–13), they gathered round Jesus and 'reported to him all they had done and taught' (verse 30). They were full of excitement as they gave their feed-back. Unfortunately their time of evaluation was interrupted by the thronging crowds. So Jesus took them away to a quiet place for rest (verse 31). We can assume that the process of assessment continued there.

A similar exercise took place when Jesus sent out seventy-two disciples on another special mission (Luke 10:1). Like the Twelve, they were to travel light and again their mission involved teaching, healing and exorcism. They witnessed amazing results! Euphoric, no doubt, with the success of their enterprise, Luke tells us that those seventy-two workers were filled with joy and said to Jesus, ' "Lord, even the demons submit to us in your name" ' (Luke 10:17). They had tasted the power of the new age!

Christ recognized that they had achieved a great victory over the demonic forces. Their mission heralded the coming defeat of Satan himself (verse 18). In his assessment, Jesus warned his followers not to exult over their phenomenal accomplishments, but to rejoice that their names were written in heaven (verse 20; see Exodus 32:32; Daniel 12:1; Revelation 3:5). He prayed, thanking his heavenly Father for revealing his will and purpose to the disciples. Then he conveyed to them their unique privilege in seeing, hearing and experiencing what their prophetic and royal forefathers had longed to see (verses 23–24).

Lessons for today

Someone has made the wry remark that 'most Christian events end with the benediction'! We breathe a sigh of relief when the conference or exhibition has come to a successful conclusion. But we miss out on a crucial factor – evaluation. This is probably one of the most important elements in training. Evaluation enables us to assess our achievements. Have we met our goals? Have participants worked effectively and harmoniously? What were the weak spots and how could these have been overcome? What have we learnt from the event that will help us to plan and make a better job of it next time? What are some of the spiritual lessons that God is teaching us? Evaluation can often pave the way for even greater exploits for God!

7 He rebuked them

At times, Jesus rebuked his disciples. Once, when they were sailing across the Lake of Galilee, their boat was caught in a furious squall. Jesus was fast asleep. Panic-stricken, the disciples cried out, ' "Teacher, don't you care if we drown?" '

(Mark 4:38). Jesus chided them for their lack of faith. He commanded the winds and the storms to cease, and within seconds all was still.

We referred earlier to Peter's confession of Jesus as the Messiah. He was commended for his declaration of faith (Matthew 16:16–17). But when Christ sought to explain his mission with its costly price of suffering, Peter rebuked him; he thought that his Master was out of his mind. Peter must have been shocked when Jesus turned on him and spoke these stern words:

'Out of my sight, Satan! You are a stumbling block to me; you do not have in mind the things of God, but the things of men' (verse 23).

Christ did not mince his words. He took Peter to task for attempting to hinder him from fulfilling his role as the suffering servant.

On their way to Jerusalem, Jesus and the Twelve had to pass through a Samaritan village (Luke 9:51–56). Because of the longstanding feud between Samaritans and Jews, the disciples, who were all Jews, met with a stony reception. James and John, the Sons of Thunder, impetuously blurted out, ' "Lord, do you want us to call fire down from heaven to destroy them?" ' (verse 54). In the minds of both brothers, what the Samaritans needed was a severe dose of judgment! But Christ turned and rebuked them (verse 55). James' and John's prejudices had to be corrected.

When Peter cut off the right ear of one of the high priest's servants, we can detect anger in the voice of Jesus: ' "No more of this!" ' (Luke 22:51; see John 18:10–11). Peter was not commended for his seemingly heroic action in defence of his Master. He was reprimanded for acting according to his baser instincts.

Jesus loved his disciples, but his love was never sentimental; he simply could not overlook sin. Christ also taught his disciples, ' "If your brother sins, rebuke him, and if he repents, forgive him" ' (Luke 17:3). Sin must be confronted, but we should remember to treat the offender as a brother. We are

85

not to act like prosecutors or judges, accusing and condemning. Love's rebuke should lead to repentance.

This truth is illustrated in the words of the risen Christ, ' "Those whom I love I *rebuke*" ' (Revelation 3:19). He exposed the lukewarmness of the Laodicean Christians and their smug, complacent attitude warranted his censure (verses 15–18). But he urged them to repent in order that they might enjoy intimate fellowship with him (verses 20–21).

Lessons for today

In our eagerness to emphasize the ministry of encouragement or affirmation, we can neglect that of rebuke. Sometimes we become emotionally charged before reproving an erring co-worker. But if we remain silent, we unwittingly retain their sins or faults in our subconscious, only for them to pop out again in unguarded conversations; thus *we* sin by gossip or back-biting! So we need to pray for courage to correct an erring brother or sister. The ministry of rebuke is best done face-to-face, the aim being for the offender to repent and be restored. This can only be achieved by 'speaking the truth *in love*' (Ephesians 4:15). When we do this, we will not crush a person's faith and dignity; on the contrary, he should feel loved and accepted.

Since we ourselves are sinful and fallible, we need to *pray* before we correct our brother or sister. Unlike Jesus who is sinless, we need the grace to accept other people's criticism. If we respond badly when someone rebukes us, they will not do so again and we shall be the losers!

8 He prayed for them

We have considered the example of Christ as a man of prayer in chapter four. We have also noted that he spent all night in prayer before appointing the Twelve. The disciples must have continually been the subjects of his prayers. We overhear him praying for them when he thanked his heavenly Father for revealing divine truths to this circle of followers (Matthew 11:25–27). But his most intimate prayer for his disciples is preserved for us in John 17. It is a poignant prayer which

86

provides us with invaluable guidelines on how to pray for our fellow leaders.

First, Jesus thanks God for his disciples (verses 6–10). He treasures the Eleven because they are the Father's gift to him. His prayer begins with this sense of gratitude.

Second, Jesus prays for their protection (verses 11–12). While he was with them they were secure, but soon he will be leaving them. They will experience the attacks of the Evil One who will stir up both the civil and religious authorities to prevent them from fulfilling their worldwide mission. Protection is not to mean insulating them from opposition and trials (verse 15). They are sent to glorify God *in* the world.

Third, Jesus prays for their sanctification (verse 17) as well as his own (verse 19). Here the word 'sanctification' implies being set apart for special service. Leon Morris offers this comment:

> Jesus sets Himself apart to do the will of God and He looks for them to be set apart to do God's will. But the implications are not the same in the two cases. For Him the consecration issued in an atoning death: for them in lives of service (sometimes crowned with the death of the martyr) (Morris 1971:731).

Fourth, Jesus focuses his prayer on the unity of his disciples. The phrase, 'that they may be one', occurs three times (verses 11, 21, 22). This unity is not uniformity or organizational oneness; it is closely linked to the Son's union with the Father (verses 21–22). Their oneness is an important witness to the world (verse 21).

Finally, Jesus expresses his deep longing that his disciples might behold his glory (verse 24) and increase in the knowledge of God (verse 26).

Lessons for today

Our prayers take on a new perspective when we begin to thank God for each of our fellow workers. They are God's gift to us. Thanksgiving opens the way for us to appreciate them and their partnership with us in the gospel. We need to pray for one another's protection because we are engaged in fierce combat against the forces of darkness. Satan will attack us and one of his favourite ploys is to divide and rule. If he can drive a wedge between leaders, he'll gain the upper hand. So prayer for unity amongst leaders is crucial.

In the heat of the battle we can be tempted to withdraw or compromise, hence the prayer for consecration. Commitment to do the will of the Father will keep us on course.

Have we ever prayed that we and our co-workers will catch a glimpse of God's glory? That prayer lifts us to new heights of spiritual experience (see Exodus 33:18–22; 2 Corinthians 3:17–18).

9 He commissioned them

Christ had almost completed his work on earth. For three years he had taught and trained his disciples; he had prepared and equipped them to be the builders of his church; he had suffered and died for the sins of the world; he had risen from the dead. The disciples had been eye-witnesses of these staggering events.

Just before he returned to the Father, he gave them this mandate:

> 'Go and make disciples of all nations, baptising them in the name of the Father and of the Son and of the Holy Spirit, and teaching them to obey everything I have commanded you' (Matthew 28:18–20).

The Great Commission begins with the Commissioner himself. Jesus is the authoritative Lord and it was he who issued the command to 'go and make disciples of all nations'. The disciples had no powerful patrons to back them in their enterprise: they went at Christ's command.

Their task of disciple-making would take them to all nations. What a radical concept! Like their fellow Jews, the disciples were parochial and chauvinistic in their outlook – salvation was for the Jews. But Christ had changed all that. They were to learn that 'God so loved the *world* that he gave his one and only son . . . ' (John 3:16).

Disciple-making, that is leading men and women to acknowledge the Lordship of Christ, required teaching new believers and incorporating them into the Christian community (symbolized by baptism). This was by no means an easy assignment, but Jesus promised the apostles his own presence (Matthew 28:20).

Lessons for today

This missionary mandate is still in force. Christ has not withdrawn or rescinded it. He calls his church, which includes us his servants, to be involved in world evangelization.

In July 1974 I was privileged to be among the first of 3,500 evangelical leaders to sign the Lausanne Covenant – an unequivocal statement on evangelism. Here is an extract from this celebrated covenant:

> We affirm that Christ sends his redeemed people into the world as the Father sent him, and that this calls for a similar deep and costly penetration of the world. We need to break out of our ecclesiastical ghettoes and permeate non-Christian society. In the Church's mission of sacrificial service, evangelism is primary. World evangelization requires the whole Church to take the whole gospel to the whole world. . . . The responsibility to evangelize belongs to the whole body of Christ. All churches should therefore be asking God and themselves what they should be doing both to reach their own area and to send missionaries to other parts of the world. The reevaluation of our missionary responsibility and role should be continuous. Thus a growing partnership of churches would develop and the universal character of Christ's Church would be more clearly exhibited.

How are *we* going to *act* on this statement?

10 He left them

At first sight this appears to be a rather strange principle in leadership training. Was three years really long enough for the disciples to learn all they needed in order to fulfil Christ's commission? Jesus had forewarned them that he was going to leave them soon after his resurrection. While he was on earth, he could only be in one place at a time. Moreover, we can assume that if he had remained, the disciples would have been more inclined to cluster round him than to disperse to the far corners of the earth and get on with the job! So Jesus left them. But he didn't leave them alone – he promised to send them another counsellor, the Holy Spirit (John 14:16–17, 26; 16:7–15). The Holy Spirit is not restricted by the barriers of time and space, but is available to all Christians everywhere all the time. On the Day of Pentecost he made himself known in a mighty way! And he has been guiding and empowering the church ever since.

Lessons for today

It is not advisable for an established leader to remain in a position of responsibility for too long. People may become too dependent on him and he may unconsciously be restricting God's work.

We *must* leave our co-workers, especially new leaders, to get on with their jobs. They will make mistakes, but they will learn through them. If we had to wait until leaders were 'one hundred per cent ready' before they embarked on their ministry, there would be a distinct lack of leaders! The best way of training is to get them to rely on the Holy Spirit and to tackle their responsibilities with his enabling.

In 1966 I recruited a group of university students to help me pioneer a Sunday school for unchurched children in a village just outside Kuala Lumpur in Malaysia. We laid on lots of different activities to catch the children's interest. The older boys loved soccer matches on Saturdays! We won their friendship and soon a good number turned up for Sunday school. We trained a core of teachers and planned our own syllabus. To our delight, after a year the Sunday school had taken root.

Then in March 1967 I was invited to join the staff team of IFES. My family and I had to move to our new base in Hong Kong. A month later, I received a letter from one of the students, now the Sunday school superintendent. 'Dear Mr. Chua,' he wrote, 'Since you left us, the work has gone from strength to strength . . .'! That was one of the greatest compliments I have ever received!

* * *

President Dwight Eisenhower once confessed that he only read two types of letters – those marked 'Urgent' and those marked 'Important'. He lamented that he spent so much time on the 'Urgent' that he had hardly any time left for the 'Important'. As leaders we face a similar temptation. We are slaves to the 'tyranny of the urgent' and we do not devote enough time to the 'important'. Like the Lord Jesus, we must place the training of leaders at the forefront of our concerns.

Chapter Seven

THE INNER LIFE OF LEADERS

Leaders are public figures. As such we occupy centre stage and all eyes are on us. We are expected to lead from the front and people look to us for direction.

This puts us in a dangerous position. To gain the respect of others, we are tempted to project an image of spirituality. I'm sure you've noticed how keen you are to drop hints that you participate regularly at prayer meetings. That makes you truly 'spiritual'. When you've been instrumental in leading someone to faith, you have a story to tell! The audience is impressed.

Hypocrisy and true spirituality

I once read a biography of a well-known missionary leader. His biographer noted that this man displayed exceptional spirituality because he would often fall on his knees and pray audibly in the presence of his guests. His biographer was completely fooled by his artificial piety!

Jesus warned us against hypocrisy. In his day, the Pharisees (ostentatiously) paraded their spirituality (see Matthew 6:1–8, 16–18). They loved to pray in public; they drew attention to their fasting. When they gave alms, their act of charity was accompanied by trumpet and fanfare. They were hypocrites.

Now the Greek word *hupokritēs* describes an actor in ancient Greece or Rome who regarded the world as his stage and himself as the central character. He would put on different masks to portray different characters. This was an accepted convention in the world of drama, but in real life, to put on a mask of piety is to be insincere. The Pharisees fell into this trap. They wanted their audience to applaud them, but the pious image they projected was a far cry from their true selves. Their false spiritual façade might have earned the praise of their fellow men, but God was not the least impressed! He saw through their pretence.

Jesus counselled his disciples to cultivate a devotional life in private, not seeking publicity or the praise of men. They were to withdraw to their rooms so that they could spend time in the presence of God. He is our unseen heavenly Father and his commendation matters far more than that of men (verse 6; see also verses 3–4, 17–18).

Sustaining our inner lives

Our inner lives are like the roots of a tree. Though hidden, strong, healthy roots sustain and nourish the trunk, branches, leaves and fruit. In times of drought, tall trees die and fall because their roots are not supplying them with vital water and nutrients. The prophet Jeremiah paints this vivid picture of a believer who is in constant touch with the Lord:

> 'But blessed is the man who
>   trusts in the LORD,
>   whose confidence is in him.
> He will be like a tree planted
>   by the water
>   that sends out its roots by
>   the stream.
> It does not fear when heat
>   comes;
>   its leaves are always
>   green.
> It has no worries in a year of
>   drought
>   and never fails to bear
>   fruit' (Jeremiah 17:7-8).

If we are not drawing fresh strength each day from the Lord, we can easily dry up. But if we want to be his fruitful servants, our union with him is vital (see John 15:1–8, 16). Leadership is exciting and exacting, and spiritual leaders have to give themselves unstintingly to meet the needs of their people. Unless our inner lives are renewed and replenished, there will be little depth to our ministry.

I have two timeless verses written on the flyleaf of one of my Bibles. I first read them in Bishop Handley Moule's volume of pastoral theology, *To My Younger Brethren* (1902:2, 22):

> Pastor, for the round of toil
>   See the toiling soul is fed;
> Shut the chamber, light the oil,
>   Break and eat the Spirit's bread;
> Life to others wouldst thou bring?
> Live thyself upon thy King. . .
>
> He that would to others give,
>   Let him take from Jesus still;
> They who deepest in Him live
>   Flow furthest at His will.

The priority of prayer

Our inner life can be built up only through daily communion with God. This means that we have to feed on his Word and be people of prayer. In this chapter we will concentrate on the prayer life of leaders.

If we are honest, we have to confess that prayer does not come easily. We find it much more conducive to run around doing things, busy with work that God has given us. At least then we can measure what we have or haven't done. We can offer countless excuses for not praying. There are a hundred and one things that need our attention. A twenty-four hour day is simply not long enough to get through our work. Many people clamour for our attention. And we feel good when we minister to people and run from one meeting to another. But we neglect the most important feature of our lives: time spent with God in worship and prayer.

It took me a long time to realize that God is more concerned with who I am than what I do. My relationship with him has to come before my service for him.

There was once a widower whose chief delight was to spend time with his only daughter. Each evening when he returned home from work, he would enjoy talking with her. Six weeks before Christmas, she decided to knit him a sweater. This was to be her surprise Christmas gift. So after supper she would retire to her room in order to get on with her knitting. On Christmas day, she knocked excitedly at his door, hugged him and proudly gave him his present. When he opened it, there were tears in his eyes – not of elation, but of sadness. The daughter asked her father why he was weeping. 'I've missed you so much during the past weeks,' he said. For him, his daughter's *presence* meant more than her present.

We need to keep our rendezvous with God. Let's never forget that he delights to meet us, and our relationship to him matters infinitely more than the work we do for him.

Our Lord urged his disciples to enter their rooms for prayer. Now the word used is *tameion*, meaning the store-room where treasures were kept. We too need to find a quiet spot where we can pour out our hearts in praise and prayer to our heavenly Father. Our prayer room is transformed into a treasure store, a royal audience chamber.

Jesus often withdrew to a quiet place for prayer. Mark records: 'Very early in the morning, while it was still dark, Jesus got up, left the house and went off to *a solitary place*, where he prayed' (Mark 1:35, emphasis mine). He chose a quiet spot so that he could be free from distractions and interruptions.

It is salutary to observe the rhythm in the life and ministry of Jesus. He worked hard, but he also withdrew to be alone with the Father. We detect an interesting balance between work and withdrawal. This was deliberate. Jesus must have felt exhausted, having spent hours teaching the crowds, training his disciples and meeting the needs of those around him. In the midst of his crowded programme, our Master never neglected communion with God.

I find it extremely profitable from time to time to spend a day or a morning in prayer and reflection. These hours are never wasted: my spiritual batteries are recharged and I gain a clearer perspective of my life and work. A friend of mine scribbles 'TWG' in his diary. These initials stand for 'Time with God'. So when asked whether he's free on a certain day, he checks his diary, and if the engagement falls on a day marked 'TWG', he can truthfully declare that he has an appointment.

Please don't just say, 'What a splendid idea!' Take definite action! Begin by setting aside a morning or evening for unhurried prayer. Find somewhere quiet and learn to enjoy God's presence. Spend time adoring him and praising him for who he is and what he has done for you. Confess specific sins and seek his cleansing. Share all your plans with him, your hopes and fears; spread your problems and needs before him. Search his Word and claim fresh strength for yourself and your ministry.

Gordon MacDonald, President of IVCF USA, has written a helpful book, *Ordering Your Private World* (published by Thomas Nelson in the USA and Highland Books in the UK). It's an excellent guide to help 'driven' workers realign their priorities in life. Follow his practical recommendations and soon your ordered life will express the beauty of God's peace.

I confess that I am an activist. I have great difficulty in praying consistently. Sometimes my mind wanders all over the world when I start to pray. It seems that in prayer my powers of association work overtime! I often wish that I had a more mystical and reflective temperament, but I have come across very few people who actually have. Prayer is a discipline; it requires hard work. But we are not left to our own strength – the Spirit helps us to pray.

Isaiah 40:29–31 are mind-boggling verses:

> He gives strength to the weary
> and increases the power of
> the weak.
> Even youths grow tired and
> weary,
> and young men stumble and
> fall;
> but those who hope in the
> LORD

>   will renew their strength.
>   They will soar on wings like
>   eagles;
>   they will run and not grow
>   weary,
>   they will walk and not be
>   faint.

What amazing promises! God pledges to give strength to the weary and weak. Those who wait upon the Lord will renew their strength. They will be like eagles soaring with grace and grandeur.

I remember once when I was swimming with a few friends in Trinidad, we watched the eagles fishing and flying around our bay. It was magnificent to see these huge birds swoop down from the skies, catching tuna fish in their mighty talons. Whenever they touched the water, they had to flap their wings furiously. They had to expend vast amounts of energy before they were airborne. But once they took off, they soared upwards, carried along by the air currents. They then flew with the greatest of ease.

For me, that was an acted parable of prayer. Like those eagles in Trinidad, it takes time and effort to achieve a lift-off.

I have learnt to quieten my heart and mind before God. In silent meditation I focus my thoughts on him, reflecting on some of his attributes – his holiness, his majesty, his covenant-love. But there are times when I simply can't get going. In my helplessness I seek the assistance of the Holy Spirit, and in a marvellous way he empowers and sets me free to praise and worship God (see Romans 8:26–27).

Praying for and with others

Leadership involves personal relationships. God calls us to work alongside our fellow labourers. Together we are to serve his people. Our objective should surely be to seek God's best for our co-workers and members.

You would have thought that the church would be the ideal place for co-operative evangelism. After all, aren't we one in

97

Christ Jesus? Are we not brothers and sisters in the same family? Don't we have the same Lord guiding our plans and decisons? The answer should be a resounding 'Yes!'. The fact of our being one in Christ is a tremendous motivation for harmonious service. But we must face the reality of human sin. This infects all human relationships, including Christian ones. Pride hinders fellowship. Failure to communicate openly with one another can easily compound misunderstandings and divisions. The unrelenting campaign of Satan to drive a wedge between Christians should drive us to greater vigilance in our dealings with others.

Committee meetings can become battlegrounds for titanic clashes between Christian leaders. Sometimes councils are ruled by power blocs with their own vested interests. I know of a church synod in Central Asia where delegates were once involved in fist fights. The police had to be called in to separate the pugilists! The situation deteriorated. The following year, some delegates attended with knives and fire-arms!

Thankfully, this story has a happy ending. The president of the synod was spiritually revived. He persuaded the delegates to devote the first day of the proceedings to prayer and fasting. To everyone's astonishment, unity and harmony were restored. Major decisions were made within a relatively short time. As they learnt to pray for one another, a spirit of mutual prayer and concern emerged.

It is always wise to integrate prayer into our committee meetings. Prayer should not be used simply to open and close meetings. A sizeable proportion of our time should be spent praying over items on the agenda, particularly leadership appointments. It's thrilling to work in a committee that knows how to pause for prayer in between items. Suppose you reach an impasse in your discussion. No solution is at hand. The leaders turn to prayer, committing the issue to God. I can't explain the mechanics, but God reveals his will and plan. As leaders we need constantly to remind one another that we are doing business for the living God.

You can gauge the spirituality of any church or group by the numbers who attend prayer meetings regularly and by the spirit of prayer. If we are in constant touch with God, we know that he delights to answer prayer. Armed with this confidence, we rally people to worship him and we present our petitions with boldness before his throne of grace.

Spiritual leaders never get tired of reminding people that they come to a God 'who is able to do immeasurably more than all we ask or imagine, according to his power that is at work within us' (Ephesians 3:20). This verse of a great hymn on prayer by John Newton rings true:

> Thou art coming to a King;
> Large petitions with thee bring;
> For his grace and power are such,
> None can ever ask too much.

Wise leaders will invest time in preparing to lead prayer meetings. Christians need repeated reminders that we worship the Sovereign Lord. He does listen to our prayers. Believers are encouraged when they receive reports of answered prayers. So we may need to tell our prayer-partners, 'Two weeks ago we prayed for. . . . God answered by. . . .'

Up-to-date news of needs in the local community and on the mission field stirs up fervent intercession. You've been praying for an unconverted family in your town and also for some missionaries serving in a resistant culture. Things take a turn for the worse: the father threatens to leave the family; one of the missionaries has hepatitis. Such news induces a greater spirit of solidarity as you seek to pray these people through their sticky situations. As leaders we should never regard prayer meetings as a drag, but as a festival of praise, and a royal court where we boldly request the King to hear our petitions for his work and people.

Leaders should covenant to pray for one another. We work best with those we pray for. Now we all know that we tend to gravitate towards certain people whom we personally like. But in most leadership teams there are a few difficult characters! We don't seem to communicate on the same wavelength; their views are diametrically opposite to ours. We can become impatient with them or even plan to resign and serve on another committee! But once we start praying for these 'difficult' fellow leaders, the Lord may put his finger on our prejudices and sinful attitudes. He will work in their lives and ours. Prayer is like oil that helps different members of the body to function smoothly together.

The pursuit of holiness

As leaders, we long for God to use us and to bless our service. But he can only use clean vessels. True, he sometimes works through us in spite of our impurities, but this is no ground for being smug and complacent. Our vision of God is seriously impaired by sin; the pure in heart see God (Matthew 5:8). Leaders are to be marked by lives of holiness. This means saying 'no' to sin and 'yes' to God. To be holy involves a renunciation of selfish and evil habits. It means yielding ourselves daily to the Lord because we are his. It has to do with the renewal and transformation of our minds and attitudes (see Romans 12:1–2) and a growing likeness to Jesus Christ (see Romans 8:29). This process of sanctification, that is, growth in holiness, requires discipline. God, the master goldsmith, refines us; he purifies us through fire so that dross is removed from our lives. But more important, the vessel becomes 'an instrument for noble purposes, made holy, useful to the Master and prepared to do any good work' (2 Timothy 2:21).

Robert Murray M'Cheyne will always be remembered as one of Scotland's godly ministers in the first half of the nineteenth century. In 1840 he wrote these words to a friend who had just been commissioned as a missionary:

Do not forget the culture of the inner man – I mean of the heart. How diligently the cavalry officer keeps his sabre clean and sharp; every stain he rubs off with the greatest care. Remember you are God's sword – his instrument – I trust a chosen vessel unto him to bear his name. In great measure, according to the purity and perfections of the instrument, will be the success. It is not great talents God blesses so much as great likeness to Jesus. A holy minister is an awful weapon in the hand of God (Bonar 1892:282).

Chapter Eight

THE AUTHORITY OF LEADERS

The subject of spiritual authority often provokes heated discussion and debate. Recently I had lunch with Ralph, and we were talking about the authority of Christian leaders. I first met him in the seventies when he was an active student radical. He had taken part in street demonstrations against political and educational authorities. Authority for him was a dirty word and he and his fellow revolutionaries were committed to expunge it and to introduce greater grass roots participation. Ralph did not stop there, for he introduced this revolt to his local church. He questioned the right of the elders to issue directives to the congregation and their insistence on maintaining rigid liturgical forms of worship. He attacked their hierarchical structure and authority base. Somehow, he and a few other Christian students managed to turn their church upside down and inside out. They even got themselves elected onto the church committee! Some of the innovations they introduced were healthy, because that church experienced greater community spirit and a larger number of members became involved in the decision-making process.

But to my amazement, Ralph explained that he had become totally disillusioned with his church set-up. He declared that all church committee meetings were a waste of time and simply ruined talents. Leaders cherished their personal viewpoints and so the vote was often split. Decision-making came to a standstill and there was hardly any progress.

Ralph had moved to another part of the country and decided to join a 'more biblical' church. He told me he was most impressed with the leaders because they wielded great authority and exercised thorough pastoral care. Every member had to be 'covered' or 'shepherded' by an older or more experienced Christian. No-one could move house or marry without the express permission of the elders. Ralph applauded this tight control. He felt like a passenger on board a ship with a captain and a crew who knew where they were going.

I told him that I'd witnessed similar authoritarian structures in other parts of the world. I related how, the last time I visited Lagos, my Nigerian host took me to his local church which was packed with worshippers. I was intrigued to find a boxed enclosure at the back with four young men in it. When my friend saw me staring at this strange piece of architecture, he smiled and whispered, 'That's the penitents' box, a kind of sin-bin! Those lads have done something wrong and that's part of their chastisement. I know one of them . . . apparently he expressed interest in a young lady without first consulting the pastor. Our pastor found out and he's now being disciplined.'

I related another incident where a young graduate in Chile approached his pastor for permission to serve as a team leader in his student movement. The pastor asked the graduate to wait outside the vestry while he prayed to seek God's will. Within minutes, my friend was called in and told he was not to assume the post. He could not question his pastor's decision because God had apparently made known his will!

I told Ralph that I had serious reservations about *authoritarian* styles of leadership in God's church. They have a form of spirituality but in reality they cripple growth and restrict the freedom of believers.

I was not questioning the right of leaders to exercise God-given authority. We rejoice when his servants proclaim his Word with authority and conviction or when they discipline members because of erroneous beliefs and scandalous behaviour. It's admirable for pastors and elders to organize caring fellowships with well-trained leaders. We are not in any way advocating a return to the dark period of the Judges where each Israelite did what was right in his own eyes (Judges 21:25). That was sheer anarchy and led to political and religious decline!

Our portraits of spiritual leaders as servants, stewards and

102

shepherds underline the concept of accountability. We do not operate as a law unto ourselves. We derive our authority from God, and this must be exercised in accordance with his authoritative Word.

The problem with authoritarian leaders is that they tend to overstep the mark. They use Scripture or church authority to bolster their own position and pronouncements. They often control and subjugate their members. The latter are forbidden to make important individual decisions without reference to them. Authoritarian leaders demand submission – their word is law. Watchman Nee, the founder of the indigenous local church movement in China, taught that whenever Christians disagree with their leaders they *ipso facto* disagree with God (see Barrs 1983:45). Such teaching breeds fear and a sense of over-dependence on leaders.

John White and Ken Blue issue this timely warning:

> Terms like covering and umbrella are often used in teaching a form of authoritarianism which has the appearance of godliness, but which is not biblical and which fosters infantilism rather than freedom and growth amongst church members (White and Blue 1985:75).

In the New Testament *all* Christians are expected to feed themselves, to discern God's will and to press on towards spiritual maturity (*e.g.* Ephesians 4:13–14; 5:15; Hebrews 5:11 – 6:2). We are even commanded to 'test the spirits to see whether they are from God, because many false prophets have gone out into the world' (1 John 4:1). Christians have the responsibility to test the teaching and authority of their leaders to see if they correspond to biblical revelation. Leaders have no right to place themselves above the authority of Scripture: they too must submit to its teaching and correction.

Recognizing spiritual authority

How do we recognize spiritual authority in leaders?

First, leaders should submit themselves to the Lord and to his Word. Their authority stems from God and they are primarily his servants, people under authority. This means that they will not aim to attract a following, nor will they bolster their leadership status by quoting select Bible texts so that their members will give them unquestioning obedience. Their lives and preaching should reflect their submission to God. They are utterly dependent on him as they seek to fulfil their ministry.

Dr Martyn Lloyd-Jones once told a remarkable story about a Welsh preacher who had been invited to address a large convention. The crowds gathered to hear him but there was no sign of the preacher. The anxious minister and elders sent a maid back to the house where the preacher was staying. The girl returned and told them, 'I didn't like to disturb him. He was talking to somebody.' They were surprised because there was nobody else in the house. So they gave her instructions to go back and tell the preacher that he must turn up for his engagement because everyone was waiting for him. The girl did as she was told but before long she returned and reported, 'He *is* talking to somebody. I heard him saying to this person, "I will not go and preach to those people if you will not come with me." ' The minister replied, 'Oh, it's all right. We had better wait.'

Dr Lloyd-Jones concluded:

> The old preacher knew that there was little purpose in his going to preach unless he knew of a certainty that the Holy Spirit was going with him and giving him authority and power. He was wise enough, and had sufficient spiritual discernment, to refuse to preach until he knew he had his authority, and that the Holy Spirit was going with him and would speak through him. You and I, however, often preach without Him, and all our cleverness and learning, and all our science and all our apologetics lead to nothing because we lack the authority of the Holy Spirit (Lloyd-Jones 1958:88).

Second, spiritual leaders will have their authority and ministry tested both by men and the forces of darkness. Those tests will reveal whether their authority is based on human patronage, self-assertion or on God and his Word.

The prophets in the Old Testament, though armed with divine authority, had their words and actions challenged by their contemporaries. Moses faced fierce opposition and was even threatened with death by his own people (Numbers 14). Aaron and Miriam contested his right and ability to lead Israel (Numbers 12:2). Jeremiah and Amos were bitterly criticized by the religious establishment when they declared the authoritative Word (*e.g.* Jeremiah 20:1-2; Amos 7:10-15). In each case God vindicated the authority of his servants.

The Lord himself, who taught with such distinctive authority (see Matthew 7:29), was rudely questioned by the chief priests and teachers of the Law: ' "Tell us by what authority you are doing these things . . . Who gave you this authority?" ' (Luke 20:2).

True authority has a way of disturbing human consciences! And their best defence is often expressed by these challenging questions: 'Who are you to say such things?'; 'On what grounds do you make that statement or set that objective?'; 'Is God speaking through you?'

Let me share a few examples.

The first relates to Charles Simeon, who for fifty-four years exercised a remarkable ministry in Cambridge. In 1782, when he was only twenty-three, he was appointed vicar of Holy Trinity Church. He expounded Scripture with both clarity and zeal. Simeon was often mocked by Cambridge society and even ostracized by his own congregation, but many students were converted through his preaching. O. R. Barclay writes:

> When he [Simeon] died in 1836 the shops were closed and about half the University came to pay their last respects. Meanwhile hundreds of young men had gone out from his influence as missionaries or ministers. When he started there was only a handful of evangelical clergy left in the Church of England; when he died it was estimated that nearly one third of the pulpits of the Church of England were in evangelical hands, and the flow of active Christians up to the University began to increase (Barclay 1977:12-13).

In the end, both critics and friends recognized that the effectiveness of Simeon's ministry was due to its being firmly based on the authority of God's Word.

The second example is that of Dwight L. Moody, the well-known American evangelist. He was brought up in a humble home and could not boast a university education. However, Moody was invited by the Christian Union at Cambridge to give a series of evangelistic addresses to town and university in November 1892.

About 1,700 students in academic cap and gown jeered and sang rowdy songs when Moody stood up to preach on the first night. But towards the end of his message, the majority were struck by the simplicity and power of the gospel. On the final evening many students went forward to receive Christ, including the ringleaders who had caused such commotion on the first evening! Because Moody relied on God and on the power of his Word, countless lives were transformed (see Barclay 1977:22–28).

The same is true of Billy Graham's evangelistic ministry. Vast audiences around the world detect the ring of authority whenever he declares, 'The Bible says . . .'. Graham repeatedly points his hearers to the living God who still speaks powerfully through his Word. As a result, thousands respond and commit their lives to Christ.

My final example relates to an incident which took place a few months ago. Two minister friends and I were asked to exorcize demons or evil spirits from a housewife. At the outset, all three of us heard a voice from one of the spirits demanding our identity: 'Who are you?' it shrieked. One of my friends replied through habit that he was the vicar of a certain church. Mocking laughter ensued: they didn't appear to respect ecclesiastical office. We immediately rebuked these spirits in the name of Christ. We engaged in a long drawn out spiritual contest, but after many hours the demons were at last cast out.

That incident illustrated the power clash between God's servants and demonic forces. Had we relied on our wits, experience and learning, that poor lady would still be in bondage. The evil spirits trembled at the authority of Christ and we his servants were able to rest on the victory that he won on the cross when he disarmed all principalities and powers (Colossians 2:15). How reassuring to know that he still gives his servant-leaders power over the forces of darkness.

Third, we recognize spiritual authority as it is demonstrated by the leader's love and example. John Stott makes this incisive comment:

> The authority by which the Christian leader leads is not power but love, not force but example, not coercion but reasoned persuasion. Leaders have power, but power is safe only in the hands of those who humble themselves to serve (Stott 1984:335).

Samuel Logan Brengle was one of the great leaders of the Salvation Army. His life and ministry touched many lives. This was how he viewed spiritual authority:

> It is not won by promotion but by many prayers and tears. It is attained by confession of sins, and much heart searching and humbling before God by self-surrender, a courageous sacrifice of every idol, a bold deathless uncompromising and uncomplaining embracing of the cross, and by an eternal, unfaltering looking unto Jesus crucified. It is not gained by seeking great things for ourselves, but rather like Paul, by counting those things that are gain to us as loss for Christ. That is a great price, but it must be unflinchingly paid by him who would not be merely a nominal but a real spiritual leader of men, a leader whose power is recognized and felt in heaven, on earth and in hell (quoted by Sanders 1967:18).

Fourth, true authority is exhibited in practical service. Paul refers to the household of Stephanas and describes its members as those who 'have devoted themselves to the service of the saints' (1 Corinthians 16:15). Therefore he urged the Corinthian Christians to submit to their leadership. The apostle also referred to two other messengers – Fortunatus and Achaicus. Together with Stephanas they had ministered to Paul, and the apostle had been greatly refreshed as a result. Such leaders deserve recognition (verse 18).

God clothes his leaders with authority to preach his Word

and to lead his people forward. We call upon his name, the source of authority and power, when we are locked in battle against the forces of darkness. We need to guard against using our God-given authority for self-promotion or brandishing it like a rod in order to subjugate others. Ours is a delegated authority; we must remember that we are accountable to the true source of authority, the Lord himself.

When leaders exercise their gifts and authority in the way God intends, others will respond enthusiastically to this exhortation:

Obey your leaders and submit to their authority. They keep watch over you as men who must give an account. Obey them so that their work will be a joy, not a burden (Hebrews 13:17).

Chapter Nine

LEADERS AND SPIRITUAL GIFTS

Christian leaders are in the business of body-building – not their own bodies but the body of Christ. The ascended Christ, like a victorious general, has generously distributed gifts to his people. Some are called to be apostles, some prophets, some evangelists and some pastors and teachers. The goal of these leaders is 'to prepare God's people for works of service, *so that the body of Christ may be built up . . .*' (Ephesians 4:11–12, emphasis mine).

The illustration here is that of a growing body with its members reaching out in service. The leader's role is not that of displaying his gifts and authority; it is in equipping God's people for service. There are two directions in Christian service: first, it is God-ward. Leaders should teach and motivate believers to worship and praise Almighty God. Through the singing of hymns and psalms and through the prayers of his saints, God is exalted. By the proclamation of his Word, the lives of his worshippers are nourished and built up. Then there is the man-ward aspect of service. Leaders equip God's people to serve the community by good works (social action) and by sharing the gospel (witness). As we serve God and our fellow men, we should expect growth.

When Paul depicts the church as the body of Christ (see Romans 12:4–5; 1 Corinthians 12:12–27; Ephesians 4:12–16; Colossians 1:18), he is not thinking of a lifeless corpse but a living organism. In the human body every limb, joint, muscle and organ are included in the process of growth. Christians as members of the body are therefore interdependent on one another and each has a part to play in its growth (1 Corinthians

12:12–27). Let's focus our attention on spiritual gifts, studying the nature and range of gifts mentioned in Scripture. Then we shall examine the special, and very important, role of leaders in identifying, facilitating and developing these gifts in their members.

The nature of spiritual gifts

The Greek word normally translated 'spiritual gifts' is *charismata*. It has its root in the word *charis* which means 'grace'; spiritual gifts are 'grace-gifts'. The Germans have grasped this concept well as they use the word *Gnadengaben*, a literal translation of 'gifts of grace'. Paul reminded the Christians in Rome: 'We have different gifts, according to the grace given us' (Romans 12:6). Therefore we should never think of spiritual gifts as prizes to be won or rewards that we deserve. They are sovereignly dispensed by our generous God:

> All these are the work of one and the same Spirit, and he gives them to each man, *just as he determines* (1 Corinthians 12:11, emphasis mine).

One question that immediately springs to mind is the relation between spiritual gifts and natural talents. How are they related? Michael Green offers this helpful perspective:

> Just as the Bible will not allow any disjunction between creation and redemption (they both hang together as complementary aspects of God's self-disclosure), so it simply does not know any disjunction between the natural and the supernatural. All truth is God's truth; all gifts are his gifts; nature and grace both stem from one Author (Green 1975:156).

Thus a man who before his conversion possesses a sympathetic nature may, when he becomes a Christian, be given the gift of encouragement to strengthen the faith of others. A gifted teacher may be given the *charisma* to expound Scripture with new depths of spiritual insight. His teaching and communicating skills will be heightened as he seeks to build up other believers.

110

Range of spiritual gifts

The following chart attempts to bring together three major lists of gifts in the New Testament.

	Romans 12:6–8	1 Corinthians 12:8–10, 28–30	Ephesians 4:11
Prophecy	x	x(2)	x
Service	x		
Teaching	x	x	x
Encouraging	x		
Contributing	x		
Leadership	x		
Showing mercy	x		
Word of wisdom		x	
Word of knowledge		x	
Faith		x	
Gifts of healing		x(2)	
Miraculous powers		x(2)	
Distinguishing spirits		x	
Tongues		x(2)	
Interpretation		x(2)	
Apostles		x	x
Counsellors/helpers		x	
Administrators		x	
Evangelists			x
Pastors			x

This list of gifts is by no means exhaustive. We might also mention the gifts of voluntary poverty (1 Corinthians 13:3), hospitality (1 Peter 4:9), celibacy (Matthew 19:12; 1 Corinthians 7:7) and craftsmanship, as illustrated by the Spirit-given skills of Bezalel (see Exodus 31:1–5). We could add the gifts of composing the words and music of cherished hymns, both traditional and contemporary. One thing is clear: there is a wide range of spiritual gifts and these are distributed amongst God's people.

Our God is described in Scripture as a God who loves variety. The apostle Peter implored his readers to administer God's grace in its various forms. The Greek word for 'various forms' is *poikilos* and literally means 'variegated' or 'many-coloured'. It is a word used to describe the multi-coloured and intricate patterns on carpets and embroidery. John Stott makes this striking comment:

> The grace of God is like an elaborate tapestry, and the rich diversity of spiritual gifts are the many threads of many colours which are interwoven to make up the beauty of the whole (Stott 1975:89–90).

We need to appreciate and treasure this all the more!

Spiritual gifts – then and now

Space forbids us to comment on each gift listed in the New Testament. It is important to note that we cannot be absolutely sure how some of them were exercised in the first-century church. Take for instance the gifts described as 'message of wisdom' and 'message of knowledge'. I looked through ten different commentaries and found eight different interpretations! Writers from the Pentecostal or charismatic tradition identify them as the gifts of supernatural insight. They cite the example of Peter, who could read the minds and hearts of Ananias and Sapphira. Thus their deception was exposed and they came under God's severe judgment (Acts 5:1–11). Exponents of this view maintain that some individuals are given a preview of future events. But other commentators, such as C. K. Barrett, interpret the messages of wisdom and knowledge as ethical instruction and the exposition of Christian doctrine (Barrett 1968:285).

Down-to-earth gifts!

Before we consider the more 'up-front' leadership gifts, we must underscore the importance of down-to-earth gifts. They may not be spectacular like the gifts of healing and tongues but they are vital in the body of Christ!

Let's reflect on the gifts of serving, encouraging, contributing to the needs of others and showing mercy (all these appear in Romans 12). Just think of Christians who week by week welcome members and newcomers to services of worship. Or those who look after the young children. Think too of those who fetch senior citizens and give them a lift to church. Or those who lovingly visit the sick, the lonely and the neglected. Consider the faithful band of workers who type, print and collate our newsletters and bulletins. What about those who generously provide hospitality? And those who give so unstint'ingly to the Lord's work? They may not be in the limelight but their gifts ensure the continuation of important Christian ministries.

Some years ago a Christian philanthropist visited me in my London office. In his gracious way he said, 'I would like to contribute . . . thousand pounds. Will you please use my gift for the training of student workers?' That sort of thing doesn't happen every day and I was so happy I couldn't contain my joy! The Lord had provided us with funds to launch our training venture!

Recently, a Christian couple shared with me the unexpected ways in which God had blessed their property development business. So they decided to establish a foundation which would support key Christian workers. They have adopted several missionaries and national workers through their venture. Such generosity extends the borders of Christian service. How we need to appreciate all these fantastic men and women with their service-gifts!

Leadership gifts

We now turn our attention to leadership gifts. Christians who possess these are not in the premier league! All gifts flow from God and because they're grace-gifts we have no room to boast. Such gifts and abilities are *for others*, for the upbuilding of Christ's body. So leaders should always ask, 'How can we use our gifts for God's glory to equip others for service?'

Apostles

' . . . first of all apostles' (1 Corinthians 12:28); why apostles first? The apostles founded local congregations and taught the infant church definitive doctrines. Paul declares that the church has been built 'on the foundation of the apostles and prophets' (Ephesians 2:20). According to John Stott, their ministry was first in time and in importance (Stott 1979:107).

The apostles were a select band of men specially appointed by Christ to plant churches and to teach with authority. The Eleven, together with James, Matthias, Paul and one or two others, *e.g.* Barnabas, belonged to this special group. Their authority was unique and they can have no successors. It's interesting that certain people in Corinth laid claim to the title of 'apostle', but their claims were rebutted because they had no right to call themselves such.

Although most Christians accept the view that the original group of apostles is irreplaceable, some believe that the apostolic ministry, just like apostolic doctrine, has been handed down from one generation of leaders to the next. They argue that the church should recognize this particular ministry. This ministry-gift is exercised by those who seek to establish churches in virgin territory. In many ways they are trail-blazers, setting guidelines for congregation life and discipline (see Prior 1985:218). David Prior also refers to the itinerant nature of this ministry and writes:

> The Holy Spirit constantly keeps some on the move in this way. They are pioneers and, by virtue of their mobility, they can encourage the wider church with their wisdom and experience (Prior 1985:219).

Eddie Gibbs, in his practical volume *I Believe in Church Growth*, compares the apostolic ministry of the first century with that of today:

> The apostles were not cautious, bureaucratic leaders, but bold, pioneering adventurers, ensuring not simply the orthodoxy of the Church, but also safeguarding its continuing

114

mobility and flexibility.

... The church needs a new generation of leaders with a truly apostolic gift of the trail-blazing kind. We need leaders who are freed from administrative and maintenance tasks ... We need leaders with time to reflect, diary-flexibility and visionary qualities who can be with the troops not just for the ceremonial parades and in the casualty stations but share in the strategic advance. They should be released to roam freely on the growing edge. Their task is as much concerned with preparing for tomorrow as preserving yesterday (Gibbs 1985:247).

Prophets

The prophets, like the apostles, were also given special authority by God. They were his spokesmen and mouthpiece and he even put words into their mouths (see Deuteronomy 18:18; Jeremiah 1:9). Their oracles began with the authoritative formula, 'Thus says the Lord'.

In the New Testament, few prophets are mentioned by name (*e.g.* Acts 11:27–28; 15:30–32; 21:10), but they usually worked within the framework of local churches (Acts 13:1), and they were noted for their ability to teach, predict, reveal and link specific believers to special tasks (Acts 11:27–28; 13:1; 1 Timothy 4:14).

They ranked second in importance to the apostles (1 Corinthians 12:28; Ephesians 4:11). Their ministry of conveying God's revelation to his people was crucial before the New Testament writings were copied and circulated.

Are there prophets today? Yes, but only in a secondary sense. As Stott rightly insists:

Nobody can presume to claim an inspiration comparable to that of the canonical prophets, or use their introductory formula 'Thus says the Lord'. If this were possible, we would have to add their words to Scripture, and the whole church would need to listen and obey (Stott 1979:161).

God does gift certain leaders with exceptional insights. He

enables them to relate and apply Scripture to contemporary issues and to specific events. Their words console, encourage and edify and there is a sense of 'immediacy' in their public and private ministry. But we must beware of prophets who claim to have a special hot-line to God; believers should weigh their words carefully because authentic prophecy never contradicts God's Word. And let's remember that those with prophetic gifts should always seek to edify and build up God's people.

Evangelists

It is true that all Christians are called to be witnesses – to share our faith with others. But God also bestows the gift of being an evangelist upon some. They are able to present the gospel with simplicity, clarity and relevance. They often help non-believers to cross the line of non-faith to faith in Christ.

Evangelists spearhead gospel advance and the church needs to release people with this gift to penetrate vast segments of our society with the good news of Christ. We shouldn't burden them with administrative tasks but should encourage them to train and mobilize others for effective outreach.

Pastor-teachers

The gift of teaching occurs in all three lists. Believers can only grow if they are properly nourished and fed by God's Word through gifted teachers.

In Ephesians 4:11, teachers are closely associated with pastors, the two nouns sharing the same article. Pastors or shepherds must be able to teach as well as to care for God's flock. We have explored this theme in the portrait of leaders as shepherds. Pastor-teachers perform a crucial function, ensuring the growth of local congregations.

Two other 'up-front' gifts

There are two other 'up-front' gifts which contribute significantly to growth, particularly in the area of organization. We tend to equate the offices of apostles, prophets, evangelists and pastor-teachers with 'spiritual' ministry. Now if these leaders lack the ability to plan, organize and preside over the affairs of their churches, how can Christians be mobilized for effective service? Paul mentions the two gifts of 'leadership' (literally 'governing', Romans 12:8) and 'administration' (1 Corinthians 12:28).

First, there is a distinct gift of leadership. The Greek word *proistamenos* conveys the picture of someone presiding over others. The position of an executive president is a good modern equivalent. The verb *proistanai* occurs in 1 Thessalonians 5:12 and 1 Timothy 5:17, where it refers to presiding over a congregation, and in 1 Timothy 3:4–5 and 12, where it refers to the governing of households.

A growing Christian community requires someone who can diligently preside over them and over their leadership team. This leader is someone who can guide meetings with great skill; he prevents leaders from getting side-tracked by urging them to tackle matters of priority. I think we can spot this gift in James when he presided so ably over the famous Council of Jerusalem (Acts 15:13–21). Professor Cranfield tells us that the verb *proistanai* can also mean 'support', 'succour' and 'protect' (Cranfield 1983:627). He suggests that this specific gift of leadership applies to the leader who defends the interests of widows, young children, newcomers and those who are sometimes overlooked by others. Thus this person acts as a conciliator, bringing reconciliation and harmony whenever conflicts arise. There is certainly scope for such leaders to exercise their gift of presiding in our churches!

What about administrators? Some Christians are rather frightened of these officers! Can they exercise *spiritual* responsibility? Paul classifies administration as a spiritual gift, so we must recognize it as such. We mustn't think of administrators as bureaucrats who inundate us with reams of paper and who are sticklers at forcing everyone to observe the minutiae of the law and the constitution. In fact, Paul uses a rather colourful word to describe the gift of administration: *kubernēsis*, which means piloting or steering. The *kubernētēs* is a helmsman whose chief task is to keep his ship on course. He's always at the helm steering his vessel away from rocks. He maps the direction of the craft; he knows its capabilities and the skill and experience of his crew. When the weather changes, he adjusts his navigational plans accordingly. What a vivid picture of an administrator!

Every church needs an able helmsman or pilot. Incidentally, modern Greek employs the same word, *kubernētēs*, for an airline pilot. Many of our congregations and organizations run round in circles and don't get anywhere, because we fail to encourage administrators to recognize the importance of this leadership gift. It is often a bad strategy to saddle the pastor (unless he has the gift of administration) with the duties of presiding at business meetings and deciding upon the necessary steps to implement over-all objectives and goals. We should call in the administrators! Some pastors and Christian workers are specially gifted for counselling (another spiritual gift), and being people-orientated, are often immersed in meeting personal needs. Eddie Gibbs makes a strong plea for spiritual leaders who can really lead and plan effectively. He contrasts these with those who concentrate on their personal ministry of counselling:

> They become so entangled in the problems of individuals that the church as a whole loses a sense of direction and lacks cohesion. A captain of a ship cannot confine himself to the sick bay. He must get back on the bridge (Gibbs 1985:281).

Most of us are familiar with the King James rendering of Proverbs 29:18. We've probably quoted it: 'Where there is no vision, the people perish.' The Septuagint (the Greek translation of the Old Testament) uses the word *kubernēsis*, so we could translate the text along these lines: 'Without administrators, the people perish.' Let's keep our eyes open for godly Christians who possess this gift.

God has endowed certain people with leadership gifts, but they are not intended for show or self-aggrandisement. They should always be channelled for the benefit and blessing of others, resulting in all our members exercising their God-given gifts. We quench the Spirit if we fail to make room for the exercise of spiritual gifts.

Identifying and developing gifts

How are leaders to identify and encourage the use of spiritual gifts in their members? Not at the regular Sunday service! Unfortunately, that is a very poor context for discovering the wide variety of gifts.

Some of our worship services appear to combine the 'lecture hall' and the 'theatre' atmosphere. Churches that stress the preaching of the Word focus their services upon the pulpit and the preacher. True, we must hear God speaking to us through his Word. But only one or two people will teach and expound Scripture.

Churches with a strong liturgical tradition feature several dramatic acts. The priests wear colourful robes, and choirs chant psalms and render exquisite musical anthems. The liturgy incorporates audience participation in set prayers and responses; the scene at the Last Supper is re-enacted at the communion table. Some churches include drama and dance. All these evoke a theatrical performance, albeit in rather spiritual and mystical dress and language. Here again only a few can play the main parts – ordained ministers, gifted organists, choir members, actors and actresses. The majority watch the performance either in awe or boredom!

I can almost hear our Pentecostal friends objecting, 'But we're quite different. Haven't you been to a charismatic service? Different people give words of prophecy and exhortation. Sometimes healing takes place. Our services are punctuated with testimonies and shouts of "Hallelujah!" Aren't we exercising our gifts at our services?' Equally, those who exercise oversight at Brethren assemblies can point to the 'open structure' of their services. Members, particularly the men, are encouraged to give a word, lead in prayer or announce a hymn.

Undeniably there is greater lay participation at these services. But if we were to keep a record of the participants, we would probably discover that it is always the same people who assume the 'public ministry'. The majority still just sing along and support the action.

There is a definite place for regular services where the Word is taught and the congregation celebrates the greatness and the

119

goodness of God. There is room for music and in some instances drama, testimonies and open praise and prayer.

All I am contending is that there is a better context for the majority of our members to discover and use their gifts and talents. I refer to the small group, variously labelled 'house group', 'Bible study group', 'fellowship group', 'cell group' and 'action group'.

Howard Snyder boldly maintains:

> A small group of eight to twelve people meeting together informally in homes is the most effective structure for the communication of the gospel in modern seculurban society . . . Methodologically speaking, the small group offers the best hope for the discovery and use of spiritual gifts and for renewal within the church (Snyder 1975:139).

Snyder goes on to illustrate the advantages of the small group structure, stressing its flexibility, mobility, openness of the members (so essential for caring) and fellowship. Small groups can be effective in reaching out in evangelism and in service. They do not require 'professional' leadership as lay members can be trained to lead. More important, the small group is 'best seen as an essential component of the church's structure and ministry, not a replacement of it' (Snyder 1975:142).

Snyder draws a lesson from church history. During the Great Evangelical Awakening in eighteenth-century England, thousands of men and women were converted through the preaching of George Whitefield and John Wesley. Wesley was a superb organizer. He realized that if the young converts were to continue in their faith, they required spiritual discipline, fellowship and encouragement. So he organized his famous *classes*, the historical precedents of the small group.

> The classes were in effect house churches . . . meeting in the various neighbourhoods where people lived . . . The classes normally met one evening each week for an hour or so. Each person reported on his or her spiritual progress, or on particular needs or problems, and received the support and prayers of the others (Snyder 1980:54–55).

These classes became the backbone of the Methodist Church. The fruit of Wesley lasted because he had developed this basic structure to cope with church growth. In addition he encouraged the formation of bands which exercised pastoral care and trained lay preachers for his preaching houses. Gifts were spotted, developed and released for effective ministry.

Moving from eighteenth-century England to a more contemporary situation, let's peek into the activities of a small group or house fellowship in Buenos Aires, Argentina. This small group had been discussing at its weekly gatherings the relationship between husbands and wives and their respective duties. One week they were discussing the theme of the husband as head of the home. Juan Carlos Ortiz, a former pastor of this church, tells the story in his own inimitable style!

'Well, Roberto!'

The leader turns to Roberto and says, 'Well, Roberto, are you really the head of your house?'

'Well, I tell you,' Roberto says, 'we've really been through a problem here lately. I guess I'm not the head of my home, because I don't know how to solve it.'

'What happened?'

'Well, my father-in-law died recently, and he had a big dog that he really loved. We had to bring my mother-in-law to live with us, and of course she had to bring along the dog, since it's a remembrance of her husband.

'The trouble is, our apartment is too small for a dog. So we argue about it. I say the dog has to go. My wife says, 'Poor mom – she's so old. The dog reminds her of daddy. Please be kind and let him stay.' We're getting nowhere – I don't even know if I want to keep living there anymore.'

Someone in the cell says, 'Listen, Roberto – I can help you. I live on the outskirts of the city, and I have a big piece of land. Let me take care of the dog for a while.'

But the leader says, 'No, Roberto, perhaps God sent the dog to your home to teach you something. Listen, you are not the head of your home – but not for the reason you think. A head is not just someone who gives orders to everybody. A

121

head is someone who brings solutions, who thinks out what needs to be done.'

'How can a dog be worth all that trouble? He's tearing the whole family apart, and he's not even a person.'

And someone else says, 'Listen, maybe the dog shouldn't be in the apartment – maybe you're right. But maybe God wants you to learn to love that dog anyway. Come on Roberto – you're losing your wife, you're making the old woman unhappy. The problem really isn't the dog – it's you.'

Roberto says, 'Oh, no. I can't!'

'Don't worry,' the leader says. 'We're going to pray for you that God will give you the power to accept the dog. Come here and sit in the middle of the room.' We all gather around and lay hands on him to pray. 'God, give him victory over the dog. Make him love his wife and his mother-in-law. Please help him . . .'

Roberto starts to weep. Finally he says, 'Okay, I think I can do it now.'

'All right,' we say. 'Now on your way home, stop in a store and buy the dog a new coat. If you don't have the money, we'll give you some. You must learn to love the dog. You are working out a solution to the problem in your home.'

What Roberto doesn't know is that at that moment his wife is with my wife in another cell. She too is telling the story of the dog. And my wife is saying, 'Listen, he is the head of your house, and you have to submit to him. Even your mother must submit to him now.

'If he says the dog goes, the dog goes. Why don't you see if you can find another place for the dog to stay, and you and your mother can still go see him once or twice a week?'

'I never thought of that,' she says. 'He really is the head, and we have to obey him. I'll talk with mom.'

She goes home and convinces her mother to give the dog away. About that time, Roberto walks in with a new coat for the dog!

You cannot accomplish things like that in a Sunday morning service.

. . . The next week we hear reports of what happened.

122

Roberto says, 'You won't believe what happened when I got home . . . !' We rejoice together (Ortiz 1975:142-4).

It is truly amazing to witness the excitement of Christians as they discover the joy of using their gifts to help others. Basically it is an experience of *koinōnia*, deep and personal fellowship.

Leaders as facilitators of gifts

There is an untapped reservoir of gifts in our churches and Christian fellowships. Our primary task as leaders is to identify and facilitate the deployment of gifts.

We have indicated that gifts can best be spotted in the context of small groups. In order to facilitate the use of gifts, leaders must list specific openings for service: unmet needs in the church and community. Our role as facilitators is to match our members' gifts with corresponding jobs.

Another aspect of facilitating involves bringing out the best in people. Andy Le Peau gives this vivid illustration:

Perhaps you've heard the commercial for Hellmann's mayonnaise. 'Bring out the Hellmann's . . . bring out the best!' The pun is apt. While claiming to be the best mayonnaise, Hellmann's suggests that it brings out the best flavors in other foods. . . . Facilitators are people who bring out the best in others. They are able to bring out the strengths in people without drawing attention to themselves. Like the mayonnaise, they may not be noticed. But without facilitators, nothing is as good (Le Peau 1983:52).

My friends in Asia and the Caribbean may not appreciate mayonnaise. For them, 'the best' is hot and spicy chilli sauce! Both sauces enhance the flavour of food.

Bash – facilitator extraordinaire

The late Rev. Eric Nash, known as 'Bash' by many of his friends, was a remarkable facilitator. When he died on 4 April 1982, his 'spiritual children' and followers included a large number of Christian politicians, officers in the armed forces, at least seven bishops, four heads of theological colleges, numerous headmasters and over 200 pastors.

Bash exercised his influential ministry by concentrating his efforts on the top thirty public schools of England (for non-British readers, public = private!). He used to hold annual summer camps for public schoolboys, and was always assisted by a team of young undergraduates, many of whom he had personally led to Christ. He had an amazing gift for spotting potential leaders and maintaining close ties with them. One such student was John Stott, to whom he wrote once a week for five years (Eddison 1984:58).

Through his quiet ministry he inspired young leaders to deeper commitment to Christ. He was rarely in the limelight but pushed forward some of his more gifted young men. No wonder God used Bash to produce so many outstanding leaders.

The church today urgently needs to re-establish the biblical norm of 'body life', where members exercise their gifts and talents for God's glory. Our obligation as leaders is to equip his people for service both in the church and in the world. The Rodoton Presbyterian Church in Darien, Connecticut, USA, has captured this spirit. On their notice-board, beneath the usual information about services, church activities and the names of the pastoral team leaders, we read these striking words:

MINISTERS: THE ENTIRE CONGREGATION

Note: the quotation from *Disciple* by Juan Carlos Ortiz, which appears on pages 121–123, is used by permission of the publishers, Creation House Publishers, Altamonte Springs, Florida, © 1975, and 1976 Marshall-Pickering, Basingstoke, England.

Chapter Ten

WORKING TOGETHER

Leadership involves people. In the previous chapter, we learned that God has generously gifted his people with talents and abilities to serve him in the church and in the world. Leaders should bring the best out of their members. They should facilitate the use of gifts.

This chapter explores the dynamics of corporate leadership. What are some of the biblical guidelines for working together? We shall also adapt helpful ideas from the world of management to our decision-making.

It's exhilarating to serve God together. For a start, we are 'God's fellow-workers' (1 Corinthians 3:9); he calls us to work together with him (2 Corinthians 6:1). Our common allegiance to him forms the basis of our working relationships. That's thrilling!

Because we are human beings, we bring into leadership our different viewpoints, prejudices and weaknesses. Of course, we also contribute by sharing our experiences and insights. Let's watch a group of leaders at work.

Say you have two or three from the business world. They'll push for sound management procedures and are keen to introduce a professional touch to Christian organization. Sitting alongside them are a couple of visionaries. These are ideas people with creative flair. They have great dreams for the church but sometimes these are not earthed in reality. Then you have the thinker/philosopher type who demands a *raison d'être* for every decision. Finally, there are leaders who are warm and caring, always thinking of people rather than events.

Now if there is mutual respect and acceptance of one

another's backgrounds and gifts, this team of leaders can enrich the ministry of their church. But if they treat one another as rivals and insist on their own way of planning, there will be chaos and division. God's work will come to a standstill.

Biblical foundations

It is extremely useful to look up the words 'one another' in a concordance, listing the verb or action that precedes this term.

We begin with Christ's command to *love* one another (John 13:34–35). It's not an option; it is his charge. This declaration is repeated in 1 John 4:10–11. We are to love one another as God in Christ has loved us. This is the basis for our working together.

To love our fellow leaders is to desire their highest good. This has staggering implications. If team members are determined to seek the highest welfare of the others, they will exercise their leadership responsibilities in an atmosphere of trust and acceptance.

In our list of 'one another' texts we are admonished not to do certain things. Warnings in Scripture are there to be heeded. So here are some:

If we love one another, we shall NOT:
- pass judgment on each other (Romans 14:13)
- 'bite' (that is, hurt) one another (Galatians 5:15)
- lie to each other (Colossians 3:9)
- slander one another (James 4:11)
- grumble against one another (James 5:9).

Positively, love aims to build people up. This goal is fulfilled by:
- accepting one another (Romans 15:7)
- serving each other in love (Galatians 5:13)
- submitting to one another (Ephesians 5:21; see 1 Peter 5:5)
- bearing with each other and forgiving one another (Colossians 3:13)
- teaching and admonishing one another (Colossians 3:16)
- encouraging or comforting one another (1 Thessalonians 4:18)
- offering hospitality to one another (1 Peter 4:9)
- praying for one another (James 5:16).

As we prayerfully study these tremendous texts and apply each exhortation to our relationships with our fellow workers, we shall discover greater harmony in the leadership team which will overflow into our Christian community.

As we serve God together, we should bear in mind another stirring call:

> And let us consider how we may spur one another on towards love and good deeds . . . . let us encourage one another (Hebrews 10:24–25).

From these biblical principles of working together, we turn now to some practical aspects of corporate leadership.

Organization matters

In a small congregation or Christian fellowship, organization is relatively simple. Because the group is small, it is fairly easy to impart vision and share job responsibilities amongst the members. If there are queries or problems, they can be swiftly ironed out.

In a community of more than sixty people, we shall need to establish stronger structures and improve communication links. Various activities run by different sets of leaders or committees need to be co-ordinated and integrated into the over-all objectives and plans of the church. The leadership team will have to present clear goals and map out the direction in which the church should travel. Thus a communication network will develop, but not without effort.

Unless we are content to allow one man – the pastor – to organize and run the whole show, leaders should pray and plan together. Members have to be mobilized for effective service. The team or committee is normally invested with authority to carry through responsibilities for the entire congregation. Team leaders monitor progress and tackle different problems that arise. But all the time they seek to challenge the entire group to maintain God-given priorities.

In the chapter entitled 'The choice of leaders', we emphasized the qualifications required of leaders. They should be men and women who are full of the Holy Spirit and full of faith and wisdom. These essential qualifications are vital for spiritual leadership. But at the same time, if they are to accomplish their tasks they must learn to make decisions together. This requires thorough planning and a certain amount of administrative skill. Leaders must know *what* needs doing, and they should consider *who* should do it and *when*.

Team leaders should spend time working through plans and thinking ahead. They will not do all the jobs themselves. Wise workers always delegate so that more people can be involved in God's work.

When we read books on management, we inevitably find a sizeable section on the topic of delegation. This is an area of leadership which is often overlooked by well-meaning Christian leaders. They work themselves to the bone and in the end collapse from sheer physical and nervous exhaustion. They fail to realize that they bring this terrible state upon themselves because they haven't delegated work to others.

Delegation

Moses had this problem. He took upon himself the awesome task of settling disputes amongst the Israelites. He was a competent judge and his people looked to him to mete out justice. All day long the people milled around him, waiting for him to pass judgment on their disputes (Exodus 18:13). And Moses almost collapsed with nervous exhaustion!

His father-in-law Jethro rescued him. This wise man warned his son-in-law against such a poor use of his time and energy. If Moses persisted in doing all the work himself, the problems of his people would crush him (verses 17–18). Jethro told Moses:

'But select capable men from all the people – men who fear God, trustworthy men who hate dishonest gain – and appoint them as officials over thousands, hundreds, fifties and tens. Have them serve as judges for the people at all times, but have them bring every difficult case to you; the simple cases they can decide themselves. That will make your load lighter, because they will share it with you' (verses 21–22).

Delegation would bring fruitful results and Moses' load would be lighter (verse 22). Sharing his administrative responsibilities would not mean that his standing as God's representative and leader would be diminished in any way. Moses would continue to represent his people before God and teach them God's laws and decrees (verses 19–20).

Ted Engstrom, in his book *The Making of a Christian Leader*, cites the benefits of delegation. There are the benefits of improved understanding and relationships between leaders and followers. People who are given the opportunity to develop their talents and latent abilities gain job satisfaction which improves their morale. At the same time, delegation eases the pressure on the leader. It frees him to think and plan strategically (Engstrom 1976:163–4). Engstrom goes on to outline six main principles of delegation:

1 Select the jobs to be delegated, and get them organized for turn-over.
2 Pick the proper person for the job.
3 Prepare and motivate the delegatee for his assignment.
4 Hand over the work, and make sure it is fully understood.
5 Encourage independence.
6 Maintain supervisory control – never relinquish the reins.

He concludes with these words: 'Never forget that effective delegation aids progress, builds morale, inspires initiative. "The final test of a leader," said Walter Lippman, "is that he leaves behind him in other men the conviction and will to carry on" ' (quoted by Engstrom 1976:165).

Failure to delegate

Why is it that some of us are so afraid to delegate work to others?

First, we are afraid that others may not do the work as well as ourselves. We are frightened of the possibility of being let down. But if we work out exactly what needs doing and assign specific responsibilities to people, they will get the job done. It is true that we have to explain the task clearly and in some cases provide training. But this yields high dividends. We will get more people involved in the work. It was John R. Mott, the well-known missionary statesman, who used to say, 'I would rather let ten men do the work than do the work of ten men.'

Second, we fail to delegate because we are afraid of losing control. Some of us become rather anxious and insecure when others have to make decisions and take the lead. We think that decision-making has been taken out of our hands. In Christian work, we need to learn to trust others. Besides, we do not lose control because if we are wise delegators we still maintain a supervisory role. Those who have been assigned a specific task are accountable to us.

Learning from the world of management?

Should Christian leaders borrow leadership patterns from the world of management? Yes, if these insights are carefully weighed and sanctified first!

Authors of management manuals and books propound their principles and share their insights based on their research and on the experiences of those who run large business corporations. Whilst we admire their goals of excellence and efficiency, we must never make these ends in themselves. We want to do a good job because it brings glory to God. To be sure, there is much that we can learn about goal-setting, the control of budgets, organizational efficiency, measuring achievements and motivating employees. However, there are fundamental differences. Big businesses can count on an army of well-trained employees. In churches we work mainly with part-time volunteers. In the world of management there's usually a chain of command; executives give orders which are to be obeyed. But in Christian service we have to inspire, influence and motivate our fellow Christians. We can't order them around like subordinates. Most churches and Christian organizations have limited funds and resources and cannot afford the back-up props of word-processors, computers and skilled secretaries. Therefore we shall need to adapt management principles and procedures to our particular situation. As God's stewards, we must seek to make the best use of all available resources and manpower.

Working together: a framework for collective decision-making

Personally, I have made good use of a framework that facilitates corporate decision-making. This framework is made up of six major components or steps as follows:

Objective   In one sentence set out clearly the main goal or aim of the venture.

Resources   List manpower, finances and equipment available to fulfil the objective.

Planning   'Planning is deciding in advance *what* should be done, *why* it should be done, *where* it should be done, *when* it should be done, *who* should do it and *how* it should be done' (Alexander 1975:17).

Communication   Communicate information to fellow leaders and members so that they become aware of the objective. Share proposed plans. Inform each person of his or her specific responsibilities. Hand out job descriptions (preferably written) so that all workers are clear about their duties.

Action   Set the plan in motion by working on assigned tasks. This should only take place when the team has followed the preceding steps. The chairman or co-ordinator may need to monitor progress and attend to organizational problems.

Evaluation   The leadership team reviews the entire programme of activities. What went well? What did not? Why not? If a similar programme were to be repeated, what would be repeated? Omitted? Have new leadership talents been spotted amongst those who participated in the venture?

This grid is invaluable for decision-making by a group of leaders. Its effectiveness rests on the willingness of all the team members to submit to its discipline. Too often a group of leaders has a vague idea of what should be done. They make hasty plans and jump straight into action, and before they know where they are there is a breakdown in communication. Participants are not clear about their specific responsibilities and to whom they are accountable. They don't see how their jobs fit into the whole. There is duplication and overlapping in some areas, while other jobs are overlooked. Exasperation and frustration set in. So leaders begin to blame one another, and a dark cloud overshadows the entire programme.

Now, for this grid to work, leaders require constant practice. They must meticulously follow the six steps.

Sometimes when I conduct workshops on leadership management, I divide participants into small teams with six or seven members in each. They have to familiarize themselves with the six steps of decision-making. Then I openly display eight or nine articles. I challenge the team members to collect ten of each article in the shortest time possible. Each item is to be carefully labelled. In outdoor situations I make use of different kinds of leaves and stones. The team that faithfully follows the six steps is normally the winner! I then allow twenty minutes for the different teams to analyse their performance, assessing their success or failure.

For the next exercise, I ask the same teams to collect twice the number of the same articles in half the time. The astonishing fact is that most teams succeed in meeting this new target. They have learnt from experience the importance of management. They have also learnt the importance of setting clear objectives, careful planning, making the best use of their manpower and resources, issuing clear job descriptions and reviewing their efforts.

Let's use this framework to plan an evangelistic outreach to be undertaken by your local church. There are nine people on the committee, of which you are one. The only 'full-time workers' are the pastor and the church secretary. Six thousand people live in your parish and your congregation has a membership of 150. How would you go about planning an evangelistic venture which would result in some folk in your neighbourhood becoming Christians and joining your church?

You may like to close the book at this point and jot down what you would do, but be sure you adhere to the six steps: objectives; resources; planning; communication; action; evaluation.

Here's an example of how one local church tackled this evangelistic outreach:

Objective   To share the good news of Jesus Christ in our neighbourhood so that the majority will be exposed to the claims of Christ, and at least a dozen will commit their lives to him. This evangelistic effort will be concentrated in a period of nine days including two weekends.

Resources   List manpower. How many Christians are able to share their faith with others?
How many Christian homes are available for informal gatherings, for example coffee parties?
What central venues, for example church hall, could be used for the main evangelistic gatherings?
Budget: estimate finances needed to pay for expenses of special speakers, leaflets, booklets, training materials, publicity, *etc*.
Are there Christians in the church who could train others in evangelism?

Planning   Work out a tentative programme for outreach. Example: two main Sunday services; evangelistic messages on Saturday evenings; special meetings for men, women and young people; coffee parties; personal

133

evangelism.
Set suitable dates.
Recommend possible speakers.
Suggest co-ordinators for various activities.
Be sure to include people responsible for training others in evangelism and also those who will organize the publicity.

Communication

First stage
Make sure that all the leaders are familiar with and thoroughly committed to this evangelistic venture.
Job descriptions should be given to specific people. Each job description should help the person to answer two basic questions: 'For what am I responsible?' and 'To whom am I responsible?'.
Second stage
Leaders should share the objective and vision of this evangelistic outreach with members of the congregation.
Prayer, finance and personal support are solicited.
Information on training programme and how each member could be involved is clearly spelt out.

Action

Before the nine days of intensive evangelism, members should be actively befriending their neighbours and sharing their faith.
Special prayer sessions should be organized.
Door-to-door visitations should be made and free gospels or evangelistic booklets given to each household.
Those responsible for publicity should get the local newspaper or radio station to publicize special events.
The main speaker should be briefed for his meetings.

The pastor, together with lay counsellors, should be available to meet with inquirers.

Evangelistic and follow-up materials should be at hand.

Those responsible for practical details (for example the arrangement of meetings, setting up the hi-fi system) should run through the procedures to avoid last-minute hiccups.

Evaluation After the venture, the committee should review the entire programme at a special meeting.

How many homes were visited?

What was the spiritual response of the community?

How could this be followed through? Perhaps two or three teams could be mobilized to visit seekers.

What about conversions? How many professed faith?

How are these to be followed up?

How should the entire church capitalize on the momentum created by the nine days of special meetings?

What gifts and abilities emerged in which members? How could these be further developed?

It would of course be immensely profitable if the findings were collated and made available to the next team to plan an evangelistic outreach. Thus the new committee could build on what their predecessors had learnt.

In his book *Managing Our Work*, Dr John Alexander made this penetrating comment:

If we want our colleagues to feel like members of one team, one of the indicators that our communications are healthy will be the tendency for our people to use the pronouns *we, our* and *us* instead of *you, your, they* and *them* when referring

135

to the organization. A danger signal may be flying when a colleague uses the plural *you* and *they* instead of *we* and *us* (Alexander 1975:65–66).

Working together should demonstrate our belonging together, and our mutual commitment to serve the same Lord. This will produce solidarity and partnership.

Chapter Eleven

A BLUEPRINT FOR GROWTH

Growth is a critical test of spiritual leadership. If we faithfully carry out our God-given tasks as servants, shepherds and stewards, and are examples to the people under our care, we should expect to see steady growth.

In certain extreme cases this may not be possible. A dedicated missionary might work for a decade in a resistant Muslim area and see very little fruit. Church growth is also almost impossible in a hostile Marxist country like Albania. But in countries where the Bible has been translated and is freely available and where there are communities of believers, effective spiritual leadership should result in both the numerical and qualitative growth of congregations and Christian fellowships.

I am always amused when Christian leaders argue and debate over the nature of church growth. Some give the impression that you can measure growth in terms of numbers and statistics. Their critics jibe, 'You may have thousands of people professing faith, but you may also be welcoming countless "pagan Christians" into your congregations.' These critics would emphasize qualitative growth and some might even object to any attempt to probe or measure this particular dimension.

Is it possible to assess growth in a certain Christian fellowship or congregation? Are there biblical criteria or guidelines?

Luke's account of the birth and expansion of the church records quantitative growth. Three thousand responded to Peter's preaching on the day of Pentecost and were baptized (Acts 2:41). The number of converts increased daily (verse 47). This phenomenal growth continued: 'More and more men and

women believed in the Lord and were added to their number'
(5:14). The church in Jerusalem encountered fierce persecution
and the Christians scattered throughout Judea and Samaria
(Acts 8:1), but this first *diaspora* of believers 'preached the
word wherever they went' (verse 4). As a result, there was a
vast turning of Samaritans to Christ.

Luke goes on to relate the remarkable ways in which the
gospel spread, especially in the Gentile world. First, the Roman
household of Cornelius the centurion was converted and bore
witness to Christ (Acts 10). However, the most dramatic
accounts of the church's expansion focus upon the tireless
efforts of Paul and his missionary team. Led and empowered
by the Holy Spirit, these men established churches throughout
the Mediterranean world.

But as Luke chronicled the spread of the Christian faith, he
also emphasized qualitative growth. He underlined the importance of teaching and grounding new believers, both Jews and
Gentiles, in apostolic teaching and doctrine (see Acts 2:42;
11:26; 14:21–22; 15:35; 20:20–21, 27).

The church at Antioch

It would be immensely valuable to track down the criteria
for corporate spiritual growth from the whole book of Acts.
However, I believe that the church in Antioch provides us with
a blueprint for growth, so I am going to identify six marks
which characterized the remarkable advance of this particular
church.

A brief background

Antioch was the third largest city in the Roman Empire, coming
after Rome and Alexandria. This Syrian sea-port was a thriving
commercial centre with a cosmopolitan population.

The church at Antioch was not founded by the apostles or
by a team of professional church-planters. It was established
through the witness of ordinary Christians, some of whom had
fled to this city because of intense persecution (Acts 11:19).
Within a short time of arrival, they began to share the good

news and 'a great number of people believed and turned to the Lord' (verse 21).

First mark: a witnessing community

We are struck by the bold and consistent witness of these Christians. Their faith was contagious. They were not campaigning for a cause, nor were they promoting a new religion. They were proclaiming Christ and summoning their contemporaries to own him as Lord. Effective Christian witness centres around the person of Christ. Men and women need to know him as their Saviour and Lord. God's hand was upon the believers at Antioch; he authenticated their testimony, and the church experienced great growth.

Today we witness the exciting phenomenon of church growth in many parts of the world. Consider South Korea. Fifteen years ago, less than 5% of the population professed to be Christians. Today, approximately 15% claim to be followers of Jesus Christ. If we were to visit Seoul, the capital city, early on a Sunday morning, we would probably get stuck in a traffic jam. These are caused by Christians travelling to church! Most church buildings are packed with worshippers. Some congregations run between five and seven services every Sunday. At each gathering, the pastor has to ask the people to come on a shift system! Stewards are specially trained to get people in and out of buildings as swiftly as possible.

In Indonesia we witness Muslims turning to Christ on a massive scale. Muslim villages have become Christian towns! This remarkable people-movement began soon after the abortive communist coup in 1965. Sociologists may identify political, economic and social upheavals as the causes of such religious hunger. God often works through these circumstances, but he has also prepared countless hearts to receive the good news of Jesus.

In neighbouring Singapore, groups of Christians who work in the commercial offices of this bustling city invite their non-Christian friends to attend special meetings or Bible studies. These activities are held in offices during the lunch hour. Christians have recently converted cinemas into churches. Local

139

churches expand by planting satellite house churches.

A few years ago the Pentecostal Church in Brazil had a million members. Today it has over seven million and two new church buildings are constructed each day! We hear reports of a large in-gathering of men and women in Africa. As the gospel is proclaimed, many are freed from their animistic beliefs and practices; they find new life and liberty in the Lord Jesus. Not only village folk, but students too, are turning in great numbers to Christ.

We must ascribe such rapid growth to the sovereign work of God's Holy Spirit. That's theologically correct. But as we observe each area, we note a common link: Christians in South Korea, Singapore, Indonesia, Brazil and Africa take advantage of their social networks to spread the gospel. They invite their friends, relatives and neighbours to churches or Bible study groups. The joyful services, spiced with spontaneous testimonies of recent converts, make local folk more aware of God. Enthusiastic Christians with contagious faith are fabulous advertisements for the gospel!

During the past year, how many have become Christians through your church or fellowship? Are our churches and fellowships witnessing communities? As we rub shoulders with our fellow employees, friends, relatives and neighbours, do we share God's love with others? Or are we like Canadian rivers in winter-time? – frozen at our mouths! How we need to pray that God will melt our cold hearts and warm them with the fire of his love so that we will share the good news with others.

There are many Christians who resent being asked the number of people who profess faith in Christ through the witness of their church. They may reply, 'Only God knows', implying that we cannot truly tell who are regenerated. Such 'theological defence' is evasive. If we do not proclaim Christ fervently and expect God's Spirit to draw men and women to him, then there will be little or no fruit. Every Christian must be encouraged to share Jesus with others and to expect God to draw them to himself.

As Christian leaders, we must not give in to the spirit of the age. Here in Europe, many Christian leaders adopt a fatalistic attitude. They shrug their shoulders and blame the post-Christian era and humanistic environment for the lack of conversions. 'People no longer believe in the supernatural. They trust science and high-tech. When they're in need, they turn to the welfare state.' These friends forget that we are in the midst of a titanic spiritual conflict. Satan blinds the eyes of unbelievers (2 Corinthians 4:4). He turns their hearts and minds to seek after false gods. Like the watchman in the prophecies of Ezekiel, we need to warn people to flee from their sin and the danger of God's judgment (see Ezekiel 3:17–21; 33:2–9). And we must preach Jesus Christ as Lord so that the God of light will shine in the darkness of human hearts (2 Corinthians 4:5–6).

Sophisticated people in this post-Christian era need to hear the gospel, but first they must meet Christians who are utterly gripped by God's love (2 Corinthians 5:14). These men and women live for Christ (verse 15). They know how to weep and pray for the lost. They claim the fabulous promise in Psalm 126:5–6:

> Those who sow in tears
>   will reap with songs of joy.
> He who goes out weeping,
>   carrying seed to sow,
> will return with songs of joy,
>   carrying sheaves with
>   him.

C.H.Spurgeon, the renowned Victorian preacher, once received a rather distraught note from a young preacher. He had been preaching for two years without seeing anyone turning to Christ. In his letter he asked Spurgeon for advice. Back came the brief reply: 'Try tears.' Tears express love and concern. But weeping turns to joy as seekers forsake sin and turn to the Saviour.

If our church or fellowship is to grow, it must be a witnessing community.

Second mark: a well-instructed community

It is always stirring to see people committing their lives to Christ. Conversion, however, marks only the beginning of their spiritual lives. They need to press on and grow in spiritual understanding and maturity.

In Acts 11:22–24, Barnabas, an outstanding Christian leader, arrived at Antioch. He was originally from Cyprus, but had been associated with the church in Jerusalem. This church sent him to Antioch to see at first hand the remarkable happenings there. God's grace was evident in people's lives. Barnabas rejoiced, and encouraged them to continue serving the Lord (verse 23). As he remained with them, this godly leader must have been overjoyed by further increase (verse 24). How exhilarating! More and more people were entering God's kingdom. They must have packed the homes and halls!

Barnabas immediately recognized that they needed to be grounded in God's Word; they had to be taught. So he sailed to Tarsus to seek out Saul (verse 25).

Saul used to be an arch-enemy of the church, but he had been marvellously converted outside the Syrian city of Damascus. It was Barnabas who first introduced the new convert Saul to the apostles – see Acts 9:27. Saul had studied under a famous scholar, Gamaliel, and this training had prepared him to be an excellent apologist and teacher. His gifts were just right for the Antioch church.

Barnabas returned with Saul to Antioch. For an entire year they taught a large number of people (Acts 11:26). The church was exposed to the systematic teaching of God's Word.

Both Barnabas and Saul recognized the importance of sound teaching. Many of their converts had come from pagan backgrounds. They needed to learn to think biblically and to adopt Christian standards. Others had been brought up in the Jewish faith. They might have the advantage of knowing the Old Testament Scriptures. But they too needed to see how these point to Jesus the promised Messiah. Both Jewish and Gentile believers needed to build their faith on sound doctrine. Like an anchor, this would prevent them from being tossed to and fro, carried by every wind of false teaching (see Ephesians 4:14).

How well taught are our members? One simple way of finding out is to notice how many open Bibles you can see at the main church service or fellowship gathering. Keen and growing Christians should want to follow the passage that is being read or expounded. We can also discover the maturity of our members by their convictions and opinions. Are they thinking *biblically*, or are their viewpoints pragmatic, merely a reflection of their culture? We have to build in systematic Christian instruction, otherwise our members will not grow towards spiritual maturity. The church in Antioch sets us a fine example because their members were well instructed.

Third mark: a caring community

Acts 11:27–30 records the prophecy of Agabus. He foretold the severe famine that hit the Roman Empire during the reign of the Emperor Claudius (verse 28). Judea was badly affected and the disciples at Antioch immediately took action. They did not hold a prayer meeting to ask God to provide for the needs of their fellow believers. They gave generously (verses 29–30) and thus exhibited care and concern. The church at Antioch was indeed a caring community.

Church historians tell us that this church was also noted for two social achievements. Some of its members opened a used-clothes store so that the needy in the city could purchase second-hand clothing cheaply. Other church members operated an employment bureau, linking the unemployed to job openings in the city. No wonder the disciples in Antioch were the first to be called Christians (verse 26). They were so much like Christ, who went about doing good (verse 26b; see Acts 10:38). Such loving care must have attracted many non-Christians in the city. The church was a community that demonstrated love. It must have made a tremendous impact.

Today we live in a world where there is very little love. Violence and hatred rock our societies. Kagawa, a well-known Japanese Christian leader, spoke of 'a famine of love'. There is hatred, hatred everywhere and not a drop of love. In this barren and loveless world, love, like an oasis, attracts. Has Christ not told his disciples, ' "All men will know that you are my disciples if you love one another" ' (John 13:35)?

Are our churches or fellowships centres of love? Do we love and serve one another? Does the local community sense that?

Or is there suspicion, fear, back-biting and tension? Can people come to us with their needs and problems, or are we too aloof and busy to care? Do we include the lonely, the aged and the handicapped in our fellowships, or are they neglected? Do single-parent families find a home in our congregations? Can the unemployed worship with dignity in our midst?

In times of spiritual revival, love is always present. Love for God draws us into caring service for one another and for the lost. At such visitations of the Holy Spirit, Christians confess specific sins to God and to those whom they have wronged. What follow are scenes of joy, because forgiveness and healing have taken place. They then experience a deep sense of belonging to God's family.

In 1960 I was in the midst of a spiritual awakening. At the beginning of that year, there were only about thirty people in our congregation, and by the end of that same year, over a hundred people had become Christians. As I look back, most of them were converted not at the main church service, but in homes and 'digs' (single rooms occupied by students). We often used to invite our non-Christian friends to our rooms and homes for meals. After we had eaten, we would sing together. Someone would lead a discussion or a brief evangelistic Bible study. Animated discussions followed. Before the day was over, two or three had committed their lives to Christ. These new Christians were drawn to the Saviour because they saw Christian love in action. The exuberant fellowship and loving service pointed many to the source of love – the Lord himself. In my travels, I have constantly observed that caring congregations or fellowships are irresistible magnets; they draw men and women to Christ.

Fourth mark: a united community

Acts 13 opens with a reference to the presence of prophets and teachers serving in the church at Antioch. There was no tension between these two offices; both ministries complemented one another. We are given an interesting list of the leaders' names. They had very different racial, social and cultural backgrounds.

First there is Barnabas, a man of faith and generosity. He

had come from Cyprus via Jerusalem. He possessed pastoral gifts. He was always encouraging others to serve the Lord and had a knack of spotting promising leaders.

Next on the list is Simeon. He had a Latin nickname, 'Niger', which means black. Simeon was either black or a man with a dark complexion. He was on the leadership team. There was no colour bar or racial segregation in the Antioch church.

The third name on the list is that of Lucius. We do not know much about him, except that he was from Cyrene in North Africa. His name indicates that he was of Roman stock. He was probably a merchant trading in the city.

Menaen was an unusual person. He was brought up in the court of Herod, which means he would have been an important civil servant. This man had professional skills and talents to offer.

Finally, there was Saul of Tarsus. Here at Antioch, God was grooming him to be the apostle to the Gentiles. His gift of teaching was deeply appreciated by the church.

We are impressed by the unity of these leaders. They worked well as a team because they knew how to pray together. The Lord was at the centre of their partnership. Someone has said, 'Unity is like a bicycle wheel. The closer the spokes are to the hub, the closer to one another.'

Some churches do not grow because of ugly divisions. Quite often these splits stem from personality clashes. There is an African proverb: 'When elephants clash, the grass gets hurt.' No wonder the apostle Paul exhorted the Christians to 'make every effort to keep the unity of the Spirit through the bond of peace' (Ephesians 4:3). Unity is not to be equated with uniformity. Christians are not manufactured from the same mould in some celestial factory! God created us differently. But there is to be harmony in diversity. The leaders at Antioch demonstrated true oneness in spite of their different gifts and backgrounds.

We live in a divided world where relationships are often fractured and fragmented. Man-made barriers of class, race and culture separate people. But the Christian gospel removes all barriers; in Christ we are adopted into God's family.

As leaders, we need to examine our partnership in the

gospel. How united is our church and our leadership team? At committee meetings, are decisions made according to different parties and blocs in our congregation? When we face controversial and sensitive issues, do we remain loyal to one another, even though we may disagree? As leaders, do we foment trouble or do we cement relationships?

Fifth mark: A worshipping community

A growing church is a worshipping community. The leaders of the Antioch church gathered for prayer and fasting (Acts 13:2). They concentrated their energies on worship and thus got their priorities right. For them, prayer wasn't something formal and perfunctory. The Greek word translated 'worshipping' was originally used of people who performed public service at their own expense. It was voluntary, not coerced. These leaders spent unhurried moments waiting in the presence of God.

The example of these leaders is an indictment on Christian leaders today. When we meet to transact business, we open and end our meetings with prayer, but reduce it to a ritual or routine. We rush to get through our agenda, and in the process we often find ourselves crossing swords with our fellow leaders. Dr John White, in his book *Excellence in Leadership*, recommends that we should divide our committee meetings in to two halves, the first to be spent in corporate worship and the second in committee work (White 1986:37).

If we honour God by worshipping together, business takes on a new light. As we wait in his presence, he speaks to us and we begin to gain a better perspective of our work and ministry. We become more sensitive to the needs of people. And God's Spirit often sharpens our minds so that we can arrive at priorities. Since God is the living Lord, he still addresses leaders today. But we must make time to listen to him. Eli the priest taught young Samuel a lovely prayer: 'Speak, LORD, for your servant is listening' (1 Samuel 3:9). Today we make a parody of this beautiful prayer. We come to God and announce, 'Listen, Lord, your servant is speaking.' We then reel off a long list of requests to him. We tell him all our plans and all the decisions we have made, and then we have the effrontery

146

to ask his blessing on them, without having first consulted the king himself.

How much time do we leaders spend in corporate prayer? If we are serious about seeking God's mind and will, let us deliberately set aside days for fasting and prayer. We can easily diagnose the health of a church or fellowship by attending its prayer meetings. How many prayer warriors are there? Is there an air of excitement and expectation as we spend time adoring and praising God, and as we unite in presenting our petitions to him? God's work advances when we, both leaders and members, are on our knees in worship and prayer.

Sixth mark: a missionary community

The Antioch church has the distinction of being the first church to become involved in cross-cultural mission. As its leaders worshipped together, the Spirit of God revealed his plan to them. They were to set apart Saul and Barnabas for a special mission.

The team of leaders could easily have protested, 'Excuse us, Holy Spirit, but are you sure that you have got the right names? Do you really mean Barnabas and Saul? We desperately need them in Antioch. After all, they are our most gifted teachers.'

The church at Antioch was willing to give its best leaders for missionary service. In partnership with the Holy Spirit, the church sent Saul and Barnabas on their way (verses 3–4). What a magnificent picture of mission! The Holy Spirit called men to a specific work; the church responded by supporting them. Both the Spirit and the Christian community were involved in that joint commissioning.

The church kept up its interest in its envoys. When Paul, Barnabas and their fellow workers returned to Antioch from their travels, the church gathered to hear the wonderful report of all that God had achieved through their missionaries (Acts 14:26–27).

The Christians in Antioch rejoiced over the way in which the Lord had 'opened the door of faith to the Gentiles' (verse 27). Their joy was marred somewhat by the Judaizers. These Jewish Christians were insisting that all Gentile believers had to submit to the Mosaic Law and in particular to circumcision (Acts 15:1). Paul and Barnabas strongly contested this line of teaching and they were appointed, together with others, to meet with the apostles and elders in Jerusalem (verse 2). Because of their missionary concern, the Antioch church requested a clear ruling from the apostles. This led to the celebrated Council of Jerusalem. At that historic gathering, Peter affirmed, ' "We believe it is through the grace of our Lord Jesus that we are saved, just as they are" ' (verse 11). Circumcision and other external rites were oppressive yokes. In his summary, James insisted, 'We should not make it difficult for the Gentiles who are turning to God' (verse 19). That historic decision was prompted by the concern of a missionary community.

No church can grow if it confines itself to its parochial interests. Every Christian should be a global Christian. Christ's final mandate points to world evangelization (see Matthew 28:19–20; Acts 1:8). We are to 'go and make disciples of all nations'. This means that we should be aware of the spiritual needs in our world today. In spite of notable advances in certain areas, there is still a huge proportion of men and women who are in spiritual darkness. About 60% of the earth's inhabitants have yet to hear a faithful presentation of Christ. The church cannot be smug and complacent; the missionary task is far from complete.

To be global Christians, we should commit ourselves to pray and work for spiritual breakthroughs among 850 million Muslims, 650 million Hindus and 1,000 million Chinese. Many of these people never come into contact with Christians. World evangelization begins with intelligent prayer. Our congregation or fellowship should adopt and support specific missionaries, and communicate regularly with them so that we can pray intelligently for their ministries.

One weak link in today's church is the relationship between supporting churches and their missionaries. The latter labour in front-line situations. They are in the thick of a gigantic spiritual battle. Every advance they make is severely contested. They become discouraged and depressed and sometimes they feel that their prayer-partners no longer care. Regular and open communication is essential. We must back them to the hilt as they seek to plant churches and carry the gospel to the unevangelized.

In 1981 the Christian Union in Edinburgh University, Scotland, decided to develop a meaningful interest in its missionaries. The student members wrote to these workers and asked them what they missed most when they were away from Britain. The CU members were astonished by the replies. Some lady missionaries were keen to know the latest fashions and fads. They were soon to return to their home base and wanted to find out the latest skirt length. In the world of fashion, skirt lengths rise and fall! Their male counterparts wrote back confessing their interest in sport, especially in following the fortunes of their favourite football teams. The CU members sprang into action! They posted women's magazines and newspaper clippings of sports articles to their missionaries. They also made a priceless discovery! British missionaries are exceptionally fond of *Marmite*, a dark vegetable extract! It wasn't easy for the missionaries to purchase this 'black gold' to spread on their bread whilst they were abroad. The students contributed generously and sent each missionary a few jars of *Marmite!* A new bond of partnership was forged as a result of this creative venture.

A missionary church gives generously to the support of the missionary enterprise. It allocates a fixed proportion of its income to work overseas.

A few years ago, my family and I spent ten wonderful days of vacation on the tiny island of Helgøy. This island is situated in a Norwegian fjord, an hour by ferry from Stavanger. It's named after the late Mr Helgøy, a Norwegian farmer. It was his practice to send a specific sum of money each year to a particular missionary society. But one year, his fruit and vegetable harvest failed and he had very little money left. He also had a wife and ten children to support! However, he determined to keep his promise to the Lord. He sent all that he had to the missionary society and exhorted his family to trust God.

The following day, Mr Helgøy and his sons went to pull in their fishing nets. Imagine their astonishment when they hauled in an enormous catch of salmon! It had never happened before in their lives! The Helgøy family sold the fish and had more than enough to live on for several months! God is indeed no man's debtor. Some years later, it was an inspiration to learn that three out of the late Mr Helgøy's ten children were now serving God as missionaries.

Finally, we need to spot and encourage members with missionary gifts and support them as they prepare for cross-cultural service. The church that is committed to world evangelization widens the horizons of its members. It introduces them to the missionary God who still loves the world today. Such missionary concern promotes healthy growth.

Summary and conclusion

We have considered the splendid example of the church in Antioch. It was a growing church because it was:
– a witnessing community
– a well-instructed community
– a caring community
– a united community
– a worshipping community
– a missionary community.

Today God challenges us afresh. If we and our churches are to grow, then like the church in Antioch, we have to be a witnessing, well-taught, caring, united, worshipping and missionary people.

Chapter Twelve

HANDLING CRISES

All leaders have their fair share of crises. Crises are in fact part and parcel of leadership.

Read the history of the church in the Acts of the Apostles. There is a crisis in almost every chapter. I remember a young Christian once saying to me, 'Wow! The Acts is full of adventure. It is marvellous to read of how God helps his people to overcome crisis after crisis.'

Some of us tend to regard crisis as something negative. It certainly can be, if we are callous in our planning habits, miss deadlines and allow a critical situation to explode. But often crises come on us unawares. They can suddenly materialize from external sources and circumstances. How should we regard crises?

危機

It is very interesting that the Chinese word 'crisis' is made up of two words – *wei ji*. The first word *wei* means 'danger' and the second word *ji* means 'opportunity'. This is indeed a vivid concept of crisis. Crisis equals danger plus opportunity.

Crisis can often make or break a spiritual leader. I recall talking to the president of a Christian fellowship. He was in the doldrums both spiritually and emotionally. Some of his members had criticized him for his lack of initiative and failure to care for the members of his committee. Recent meetings had been badly run and attendances had slumped. His immediate reaction was to resign as president. But he lamented, 'I've given so much of my spare time to the CU. It wasn't my fault when the secretary forgot to confirm the invitation to the speaker. Besides, we have all been so busy writing essays and trying to keep our heads above the flood of academic work.'

I could see the red lights flashing. A young leader was about to go under unless he could see his crisis as a test of faith.

I was thankful that I was able to counsel him to look at his problems squarely. He and the other committee members should admit their shortcomings, improve their communication and pray through this critical period. He was thrilled to realize that God was providing an opportunity for him to learn how to handle the situation. By acting wisely, he would grow in spiritual maturity.

We don't have to go down under crisis. This doesn't mean that we should be blind to the dangers and problems that every crisis inevitably brings. We can, however, welcome them as opportunities to prove God, by resolving the crises with his wisdom, power and grace.

Consider David. Whilst he was running away from King Saul, he and his band of warriors took shelter with the Philistines in Ziklag. The Amalekites raided this city, burnt it and captured the inhabitants, together with the women and children of David's task-force (1 Samuel 30:1–3).

These soldiers wept (verse 4). Afterwards some spoke of stoning David (verse 6). That precipitated a crisis of confidence. His life was threatened. What would you have done? Run for your life to escape the fury of your followers?

David did something which every man of God should do. He 'found strength in the LORD his God' (verse 6). He didn't begin by solving his own problems. He went straight to God. He drew fresh courage from him. Then with the help of Abiathar, the priest, David sought specific guidance from God.

This episode had a happy ending. David and his men were able to rescue all the captives of the Amalekites. Without doubt, his esteem would have risen among his soldiers. But I am sure that they would always have remembered him as the man who in the face of crisis found his encouragement in God.

In Acts chapters 3 and 4 we read of Peter and John being imprisoned and harassed by the religious authorities. The very existence and survival of the infant church was at risk, when suddenly they were released. They joined their companions and the first thing they did to celebrate their deliverance was to hold a large prayer meeting. The church had been through a crisis – two of their leaders had been imprisoned and attacked. The Jewish leaders would soon use their religious and political muscles to crush believers. Crisis loomed large. But their prayer was one of confidence. It was to the Sovereign Lord that they addressed their concerns and petitions (Acts 4:24). They didn't pray for their safety. Instead they asked God to enable them to speak his Word with great boldness (verse 29). This prayer meeting had an earth-shaking effect. The building was rocked by a tremor. Believers 'were all filled with the Holy Spirit and spoke the word of God boldly' (verse 31).

We must not allow the enemies of God to intimidate or discourage us. Every step that we take as spiritual leaders will be challenged by Satan and his demonic forces. And so often they use unwitting human pawns to carry out their assaults against God's people.

We find this happening to Nehemiah. God had sent him back to Jerusalem to rebuild the broken walls. He was a tireless organizer and administrator. He was able to galvanize teams of men and women to build and defend the city walls. His enemies, headed by three powerful figures, Sanballat, Tobiah and Geshem, conspired against him. What tactics did they employ? What were some of the major crises that they stirred up?

In one period during the reconstruction of the walls, Nehemiah faced at least four major crises. All these impinged on his leadership. Let's look at how he coped.

Economic and social injustice

The first crisis he had to face was one of economic and social injustice.

Chapter 5 begins with a protest from the work-force, goaded on by their wives. They were heavily committed to the rebuilding of the walls. This meant that they were not able to cultivate their farms. The result was a loss of income and a scarcity of food. The problem was further intensified by a population explosion: 'We and our sons and daughters are numerous' (verse 2). Moreover, there was high inflation. Their lands were mortgaged and loans had to be repaid (verses 3–4). They complained about heavy taxation which compounded their problems and sent them deeper into debt (verse 4). For some the only solution open to them was to sell their children as slaves (verse 5).

How did Nehemiah handle this crisis? Did he look to God and pray over it? Did he dismiss the complaints by reminding the people that priority should be given to restoring and repairing the walls? Not at all. He was very angry (verse 6). He exploded with rage and fury. But he did not take impulsive action.

In fact, he gave himself breathing space. He reflected before he spoke. Some of us speak before we think. Others may suppress their emotion and work for compromise. Nehemiah pondered the problems in his mind: 'I took counsel with myself' (verse 7, RSV). Then he accused the nobles and officials of committing social and economic sins against the poor. They had charged excessive interest (verse 7); they had kept God's people, their kinsmen, under slavery, which was totally against the Law (verse 8); their ethical behaviour and standards were utterly improper and they had neglected to walk in the fear of God (verse 9).

Spiritual leaders must not be like the proverbial ostriches that bury their heads in the sand when confronted with a tricky or dangerous situation. We must carefully investigate complaints. We can then confront offenders with facts, not with opinions or hearsay evidence. Leaders need moral courage to tackle the sins of God's people.

Nehemiah did not mince his words: ' "What you are doing is not right" ' (verse 9). So those guilty of economic and social oppression agreed to redress their wrongs (verse 12). Sin was exposed and confessed, and there was repentance. As a result, there was joy amongst the people (verse 13).

Personal promotion

The second crisis was rather a strange one. It had to do with personal promotion (Nehemiah 5:14–19). Nehemiah was appointed governor – a position with tremendous privileges and responsibilities. Every promotion inherently breeds danger. Transition to a higher rank can often tempt the Christian leader to be proud. He discovers that his position commands respect and he is consulted by others. He has an important say in the financial operations of his church or organization. He has the opportunity to feather his own nest.

Nehemiah, in addition to receiving his salary from the royal treasury, was entitled to impose taxes on his subjects. This was a practice adopted by other governors (verse 15). They often lined their own pockets. They acted as patrons in giving jobs to their favourites. Nepotism was the name of the game.

How did Nehemiah respond to this subtle crisis? First, he devoted himself to completing his task of rebuilding the walls. He didn't ask workers to transfer their energies to another project. He could have asked them to build him a palace.

Nehemiah didn't add new taxes because the people were poor. He generously provided hospitality for his guests, but did not charge entertainment expenses to his people (verses 17–18).

Why didn't Nehemiah exploit his position as governor? No-one would have questioned his action. We have an answer in the second part of verse 15: 'Out of reverence for God I did not act like that.' His generosity demonstrated his social compassion: he cared for the people he served (verse 18). There was no base or ulterior motive like canvassing votes or gaining the support of his people! Nehemiah's chief concern was to win the approval of God (verse 19).

It is said that 'adversity is the best teacher'. In times of trials and difficulties, we have to trust and rely on God. But what happens where there is prosperity and promotion? It is so easy to forget God. No wonder Thomas Carlyle once wrote, 'Only one in a hundred pass the test of prosperity.'

Should God confer on us greater leadership responsibilities or promotion, we need to remind ourselves all the more that we are accountable to him. His approval matters more than all

155

the privileges and power that society or the church can confer on us.

The threats of his enemies

The third crisis that Nehemiah had to face was the persistent threats of his arch-enemies (Nehemiah 6). Sanballat, Tobiah and Geshem cast their shadows on Nehemiah's plans and activities. They proposed a summit meeting at Ono, a village equidistant from Samaria (their headquarters) and Jerusalem (Nehemiah's base). It would take a whole day for both parties to travel to Ono.

The intention of his enemies was clear. They were not keen to negotiate a settlement; they simply wanted to impose their terms on Nehemiah or assassinate him (verse 2).

What was Nehemiah's reply? If he had spoken English, he would probably have said, 'Ono? – Oh no!'

He had a massive assignment to complete, and there was no time for such consultations (verse 3). But his enemies would not leave him alone. They repeated their request four times (verse 4), and would not take 'no' for an answer. On the fifth occasion, Sanballat despatched his personal assistant with a letter (verse 5). This time the message was clear. Nehemiah was falsely accused of fomenting a rebellion (verses 6–7). 'Lies, lies, lies – a pack of lies,' was how Nehemiah treated the evil fabrication (verse 8). Why did these men threaten Nehemiah? Their avowed purpose was to discourage him and to weaken the morale of his men (verse 9). They stooped to every possible dirty trick.

The enemies of God's servants may be compared with a cobra. This deadly-poisonous snake rises above the ground with its hood spread out. It hisses menacingly. Its formidable appearance and loud hiss paralyse the poor rabbit or mouse. Satan's nefarious allies use every unscrupulous ploy to intimidate the Lord's servants, but we must not give in to fear.

Leaders who are valiant for truth and who faithfully serve God will discover that they have enemies. Sometimes we are terrified by the opposition because of its power and experience. Nehemiah did not give in to his enemies' hostile manoeuvres. He countered their threat by turning to God: ' "Now strengthen my hands" ' (verse 9). He had no other resources but to cast himself on the Lord. Wonder of wonders! Nehemiah discovered, and we too can experience, the reality of God fighting for us and standing by us. We can echo the words of the apostle Paul: 'If God is for us, who can be against us?' (Romans 8:31).

Religious pressure to compromise

The fourth crisis was that of religious pressure. Prophets and priests commanded respect and influence. Nehemiah couldn't ignore their words, especially if they invoked religious oaths.

Doesn't that remind us of people who say, 'It is the will of God to do this or that. You support my mission, otherwise . . .'? Sanballat's cohorts made use of Shemaiah, a prophet who was confined to his home (verse 10). He may have been disabled or perhaps he was simply there because of ritual pollution.

It is interesting that the Jerusalem Bible translates his words as a couplet:

'For they are coming to kill you,
   For they are coming to kill you tonight' (verse 10).

Such a prophecy with its predictive sting could be shattering. Shemaiah proposed an evening rendezvous in the temple. There Nehemiah could be assured of a safe sanctuary.

Nehemiah saw through his cover. ' "Should a man like me run away?" ' he asked (verse 11). What a powerful rhetorical question! Nehemiah was God's man. He would not play the coward. Compromise? Never! He was not going to be lured by false prophecy (verse 12–13). A thousand 'no's' to negotiations with God's enemies!

When we are faced with a crisis that emanates from religious pressure, the easiest option is to throw in the towel and compromise. It is very difficult to hold our ground. We can be so preoccupied with our own safety that we enter into a pact of convenience. We compromise. But Nehemiah was no quitter. He regarded compromise and cowardice as unthinkable sins (verses 11–13).

I always feel inspired when I read the book of Nehemiah. This leader was a man of tremendous vision and drive. He could motivate people to tackle and complete hazardous assignments. He faced adversity; he was no stranger to danger. His enemies haunted him and gave him no peace. They employed every kind of tactic to destroy his credibility and frustrate his mission. But he stood firm. He served God and his people with outstanding moral courage. Crisis made a great leader of Nehemiah.

Financial crises

One of the practical duties of leaders is to ensure that there are adequate funds and resources to maintain and develop the work that God has given us. Many Christian organizations have buckled and folded up because of the recent economic recession. Some are still struggling for survival. Others have drastically reduced their task-force and trimmed their ministries. So why does a bountiful God allow his people to suffer grave financial crises?

Sometimes he permits it to make us review our priorities. Or he may want us to rely afresh on him and not on our methods of fund-raising, even if it means praying in our income. The principle of living by faith is a noble way to prove God in supplying our needs. The danger is that we glory in the principle rather than in the faithfulness of God. So God may withhold financial provision to teach us to rely on him alone.

But does faith in an all-sufficient God exclude the teaching and practice of biblical stewardship? Any church or organization that constantly faces acute financial shortages (*e.g.* when it is unable to pay the basic salaries of its workers) should re-examine its policy. Could God not be pointing his finger at our failure to expound the biblical principles of stewardship? Some of us may inadvertently be responsible for creating a financial crisis.

Both Old and New Testaments command God's people to tithe and to give liberally and sacrificially (*e.g.* Malachi 3:8–10; 1 Corinthians 16:1–2; 2 Corinthians 8 – 9). If we teach systematically from God's Word, we cannot evade the responsibility of his people to give to his work.

I once had to give a series of expositions on Malachi and 2 Corinthians. I had not been intending to preach on giving, but the biblical data demanded that I tackle the down-to-earth practice of stewardship. The mark of a faithful teacher is that he applies God's Word and bids his people to respond with obedience. Regular, liberal and sacrificial giving are expressions of our commitment to Jesus Christ. Should we not challenge people to give in this way so that God can pour down his blessing upon us?

Some years ago I spoke to a group of Christian students in Mexico. I was encouraging them to support their national Christian movement. But one of the leaders interrupted me and told me that very few Mexican believers tithe. Besides, in some evangelical churches in the country, any reference to money was deemed 'unspiritual'. He then asked how they could persuade Christians to give tangibly to God's work.

I invited them to look at the connection between 1 Corinthians 16:1 and chapter 15. They knew that the latter passage dealt with the sublime doctrine of Christ's resurrection and the hope of immortality. What struck the Mexican students was the matter-of-fact approach of the apostle Paul on the subject of money: 'Now about the *collection* for God's people . . .'. For him, reference to the collection was not out of place. He advised his readers to set aside a sum of money on the first day of each week and arrange for the offering to be collected (1 Corinthians 16:2). Financial crises can be avoided if leaders teach biblical stewardship and set an example in giving.

Growth crises

When a Christian fellowship or a church grows, it is always accompanied by growth pangs. These can often trigger off a series of crises.

The church in Jerusalem encountered a critical situation. There was rapid growth in the early Christian community (Acts 6:1). An emergency suddenly developed. The Greek-speaking Jews complained that their widows were being overlooked in the daily distribution of food. They were probably giving vent to their frustrations on members of the Aramaic-speaking community.

On the surface, it looked as if a racial crisis was about to explode – a very ugly spectacle. Fallen man has a propensity to use racism as a scapegoat. If we can't get along with somebody from a different ethnic or linguistic group, we emphasize this difference. And the devil knows that racial tensions can easily cause catastrophic rifts.

The apostles were naturally concerned. They summoned the disciples together. They began by stressing that their primary tasks were the ministry of God's Word and prayer (verses 2 and 4). They could easily have bitten off more than they could chew by taking charge of the food rations, hoping that this might improve relations with the Greek-speaking Jewish community. But as wise leaders, they maintained their priorities. They did, however, recognize the validity of the complaints. They were not side-tracked from their particular priorities in order to deal with a pressing problem. Instead they multiplied ministries. The Greek-speaking congregation was asked to choose seven men full of the Holy Spirit and wisdom, to handle this administrative chore. Organization – this was the solution! The Twelve publicly commissioned the seven new workers for this service, and a crisis was averted. The result was most gratifying: 'So the word of God spread. The number of disciples in Jerusalem increased rapidly and a large number of priests became obedient to the faith' (verse 7).

Coping with other people's crises

Caring leaders will often find themselves sharing the burdens of those who are facing various trials and traumas. This can be emotionally draining. Think of the pastor who has just buried one of his church officers, the husband of a young wife and father of two children who now face a bleak future. Helping a young widow to cope with her bereavement and the struggle to bring up her children on her own can be a crushing responsibility. Sensitive leaders identify naturally with those who have lost their jobs. They are pained by news of wives who have been deserted by their husbands. They find themselves getting tense as they attempt to help teenage children dabbling in hard drugs and to support their families. We should do all we can to support those in dire straits. But in sharing other people's burdens, their cares can often become ours. Before long we find ourselves collapsing under these heavy loads.

I shall never forget the wise counsel offered by a godly leader to his theological students. He said, 'We should always take other people's burdens to heart, but we must never keep them in our hearts.' We are to cast our burdens upon the Lord: he is the great burden-bearer (1 Peter 5:7).

Finally, crisis, in whatever form, should be resolved with prayer and courage. We are not to avoid critical situations. They may spell danger; we need to be conscious of their warning lights. So let's remember the Chinese concept of crisis: opportunity exists side by side with danger. The Lord provides us with opportunities to prove his faithfulness. Every crisis is a test for leaders. They do not need to break us: in fact, they can make us stronger men and women of God.

Chapter Thirteen

LEADERS ARE HUMAN TOO!

When I was fifteen, like all teenagers I had my fair share of spots. One day three close friends suggested that we should have a group photograph taken. By a unanimous decision we headed for a photographic studio renowned for its touching-up technique. The end result was that four spotty lads saw themselves de-pimpled! Careful lighting and a skilled hand had produced four fair faces with incredibly smooth skin! We never saw the actual proof, but we were more than happy to buy several copies of this 'revised' version.

Politicians and leaders in industry are also very 'image-conscious'. They hire public relations consultants to help them project the right image to the public.

Political commentators attributed Richard Nixon's failure to win the 1960 presidential elections to his poor TV showing against the winner, John F. Kennedy. One nation-wide televised debate between the two candidates made the vital difference. So next time he stood for president in 1968, Mr Nixon engaged Professor Marshall McLuhan, the 'guru' of communication, to assist him in his campaign. With careful coaching, Nixon's image of a sly and impersonal lawyer was transformed to that of a wise and caring statesman. 'Get the voters to love you!' was the simple formula. And it worked!

Oliver Cromwell makes a striking contrast to modern leaders. Witness his famous words to the artist, Mr Lely:

Mr Lely, I desire you would use all your skill to paint my picture truly like me, and not flatter me at all; but remark all these roughnesses, pimples, warts and everything as you

162

see me, otherwise I will never pay a farthing for it.

Pimples, warts and everything. . . . Cromwell was a brave and honest man. Mr Lely's portrait ought to be put on view in the gallery of biblical leadership, as it highlights Cromwell's virtues of transparency and honesty.

Bible characters – warts and all

The Scriptures do not gloss over the weaknesses of spiritual leaders. Just consider the following big names!

Abraham, the father of faith, told blatant lies regarding his wife Sarah. He introduced her as his sister rather than his wife on two occasions, once to Pharaoh's officials and the other time to a chieftain, Abimelech (Genesis 12:11–13; 20:2).

David, a man after God's own heart (see Acts 13:22), was guilty of adultery, cover-up and murder (2 Samuel 11). The prophet Nathan openly confronted him with his crimes (12:1–12). Humbled, David confessed his sin, repented and was restored to God (verse 13). Even David wasn't perfect.

Jonah tried to run away from God, fleeing from his responsibility to proclaim God's message to the people of Nineveh (Jonah 1:1–3). He is vividly portrayed as a disobedient servant, who thought God's love for people was restricted to his own countrymen, the Jews.

Simon Peter is colourfully depicted in the gospels as an impulsive character. His words always ran ahead of his thoughts. On the one hand he could confess Jesus as the Messiah, the Son of the living God (Matthew 16:16); on the other, he wrongly (if innocently) tried to deflect his master from the cross (verse 22). In a single night he could both rashly swear allegiance to Christ, loudly announcing that he would never forsake his Lord, and yet also deny Jesus three times. Peter was clearly shown through a vision that the Gentiles were to be welcomed into God's kingdom and church without having to become Jews, but he later compromised, probably because of the lobbying of the Judaizers. He dissociated himself from the Gentiles and it took another apostle, Paul, to denounce his actions and attitude (Galatians 2:11–13).

Then there is the fascinating case of the young leader John Mark. It was in his home that the leaders of the early church used to gather for prayer. Later he was chosen to accompany Paul and Barnabas on their epic missionary journey. Within weeks, young Mark had left the missionary band to return to Jerusalem (Acts 13:13). He had let the team down. He was a 'failure'. Paul did not quickly forget that. When his colleague Barnabas wanted to take John Mark with them on the second missionary journey, Paul refused. 'Deserter, deserter', was etched in the mind of Paul (Acts 15:38). We know the sad sequel. Paul quarrelled with Barnabas and the latter took Mark to Cyprus.

From church history we learn that Mark later became an important leader in the early church. The church in Egypt made him its patron saint. It is commonly accepted that it was Mark who recorded the apostle Peter's memoirs in the second gospel. Initially he might have been branded a failure and a deserter. But Paul later adopted a very different attitude towards him. Mark is included in the list of men who sent greetings to the church in Colossae (Colossians 4:10), and the ageing apostle insisted that Timothy should take Mark with him, 'because he is helpful to me in my ministry' (2 Timothy 4:11). John Mark's failure was not swept under the carpet. Like all spiritual leaders, he needed to mature. But forgiveness and reconciliation won the day.

In a world of fierce competition there is little room for faltering leaders. However, while the slogan, 'The survival of the fittest', rings true in the secular world, it does not apply in the community of Christ. Mark's failure was never ultimate. He was restored to a position of leadership.

Let us never forget that Christ forgave Peter and the other apostles who had forsaken him in the hour of trial. He went on to entrust to them the responsibility of continuing his mission on earth (Matthew 28:18–20; Acts 1:8).

Just because we are leaders, we shouldn't hide our weaknesses. We are human and sinful creatures. Satan won't let us forget our misdeeds and he stresses the gravity of our sins. For once, the father of lies appears to be telling the truth! But he would like to see us wallowing and floundering in the Slough of Despond. He subtly insinuates that our sins disqualify us from divine service. Don't listen to him! Someone has wisely said, 'The great sin is not to sin and fall, but to sin and never rise again.'

Remember, Satan wants to keep us in the miry pit of failure and self-pity for as long as possible. He is jubilant when leaders remain in a state of self-recrimination and inactivity. So how do we rise again? I have found a passage in Micah chapter 7 extremely practical and reassuring. The downcast leader can turn to the Evil One and echo the words of the prophet Micah (verses 8–9):

> Do not gloat over me, my
>   enemy!
> Though I have fallen, I will
>   rise.
> Though I sit in darkness,
>   the LORD will be my light.
> Because I have sinned against
>   him,
>   I will bear the LORD's wrath,
> until he pleads my case
>   and establishes my right.
> He will bring me out into the
>   light;
>   I will see his justice.

In our darkness and despair we can look to God for light. We are privileged to live in God's economy of grace, so confessing our sins, we can also claim the promise in 1 John 1:8–9:

> If we claim to be without sin, we deceive ourselves and the truth is not in us. If we confess our sins, he is faithful and just and will forgive us our sins and purify us from all unrighteousness.

We admit our sins, we cry to him for forgiveness and we are *promised* that the blood of Jesus purifies us from *every* sin (verse 7). Our fellowship with God is restored. Returning to the passage in Micah, the chapter ends with two wonderful verses (18–19):

> Who is a God like you,
>   who pardons sin and
>   forgives the transgression
>   of the remnant of his
>   inheritance?
> You do not stay angry for ever
>   but delight to show
>   mercy.
> You will again have
>   compassion on us;
>   you will tread our sins
>   underfoot
>   and hurl all our iniquities into the
>   depths of the sea.

We can never fully comprehend the amazing grace and compassion of God. He hates sin, but *delights* to show mercy. He hurls our iniquities into the depths of the sea. We must not allow past sins that have been confessed and forgiven to hamper our progress. I shall never forget the words of an evangelist who told the crowd, 'When God buries our sins in the depths of the deep blue sea, he also erects a sign on land – "No fishing allowed".'

Leaders are fragile – handle with prayer

Leaders are not spiritual 'supermen' or 'wonderwomen'. Some are plagued with physical weaknesses. In 2 Corinthians, Paul lifts the lid off his personal life and shares with his readers the severe trials which he has encountered: hard labour, frequent imprisonments, severe floggings, constant exposure to death, stoning, three shipwrecks, sleepless nights, hunger and thirst, and all kinds of deprivation (11:23–29). All these had left him totally weak (verse 29).

To make things worse, he was plagued with 'a thorn in my flesh' (12:7). He asked the Lord to remove this painful disability (12:8). However, his request was turned down on three occasions. Yet Paul chose to boast of his weaknesses (12:5, 9–10). Was he a masochist, glorying in physical punishment and affliction? No! He was simply glad to have an opportunity to testify to the grace of God. God upheld Paul in his suffering. His healing words were a source of tremendous assurance and comfort for Paul:

'My grace is sufficient for you, for my power is made perfect in weakness' (verse 9).

Paul's weaknesses made him rely all the more on the power and strength of Christ.

In the same letter, Paul also reminds us that the gospel treasure is housed in jars of clay (4:7). This treasure, defined as God's light reflected in the face of Christ and penetrating and transforming human hearts (verse 6), demonstrates the all-surpassing power of God. It is dynamite! But the carriers of this gospel light are fragile earthen jars. These were inexpensive house-lamps, easily damaged and prone to crack. That is the picture of us. Sometimes we are 'hard pressed on every side, but not crushed; perplexed, but not in despair' (verse 8). These clay pots do not draw attention to themselves. They may be weak and fragile, but it is the radiance of God's light that matters. It spells spiritual power and glory. We want everybody to be attracted to *Christ*, the light of the world, and to follow him (John 8:12). We do not need to apologize for our weakness and frailty – that is part of our human nature.

When we recognize our weakness and also the immeasurable power of God, we naturally want to know God's all-sufficient grace in our lives. We have spoken about our need to rely fully on him. Our weakness should also prompt us to ask others to pray for us. Paul was a spiritual giant, yet he repeatedly asked his readers to pray for him. Listen to his appeals:

Pray also for me, that whenever I open my mouth, words may be given me so that I will fearlessly make known the mystery of the gospel, for which I am an ambassador in chains. Pray that I may declare it fearlessly, as I should (Ephesians 6:19–20).

Devote yourselves to prayer, being watchful and thankful.

And pray for us, too, that God may open a door for our message, so that we may proclaim the mystery of Christ, for which I am in chains. Pray that I may proclaim it clearly, as I should (Colossians 4:2–4).

Brothers, pray for us (1 Thessalonians 5:25).

So let us entreat others to intercede for us. We will discover that they will pray more earnestly for us if they know that we stand in need of God's grace and strength.

Sharing our weaknesses

Some years ago I was ministering to a group of students and graduates in West Malaysia. It was the end of the conference. We shared our concerns and asked for prayer. I was relatively new to student work at the time and told them of the anguish that I suffered at having to leave my wife and our first child at home on their own. There were tears in my eyes as I spoke of how much I missed them. I also shared the tensions I felt in relating to rich relatives in Singapore who thought I was crazy to be in full-time Christian work. I asked the students to remember me in their prayers. Afterwards, two students came up and said something that I have never forgotten: 'We thought that Christian leaders never cried or felt homesick. We thought you had no trouble in making heroic sacrifices. Now that you've opened your heart to us, we promise to pray for you every day.' I realized that they had put me on a spiritual pedestal. They assumed that Christian leaders were a super-breed, immune from temptations, trials, pains and buffetings. So it is by sharing our struggles that we help others to pray for us. No Christian leader can exercise a fruitful ministry if he doesn't enjoy the supportive fellowship of faithful prayer warriors.

In most societies the weak are either overlooked or trampled on. It is a great temptation for Christian leaders to run down fellow leaders. We think we can add a few feathers to our cap if we point out faults in others. So how should we treat leaders who have momentarily lapsed or sinned? Paul's exhortation to the Galatian Christians still applies: 'Brothers, if someone is caught in a sin, you who are spiritual should restore him gently. But watch yourself, or you also may be tempted' (Galatians 6:1). The verb 'restore' is used in Greek of mending nets and of putting a dislocated bone back in its place. Our fellow leaders are part of the same network and body, and we have the task of mending and restoring them. The fact that they are human and vulnerable should stir us to pray for them, and they for us.

Once, when I was feeling rather depressed, I began to harbour negative feelings against my fellow leaders. Our perspective of people is distorted when we are in the trough of despondency! Frictions can often erupt. I became acutely aware of the faults of my co-workers. I had expected them to be shock-proof and almost perfect. Whilst brooding over these negative thoughts, I read Dr Lewis Smedes' sermon on our vulnerability as messengers of the gospel. We may house the most wonderful treasure – the gospel itself – but we are still jars of clay. Smedes comments:

The finest pieces are sensitive, easily chipped, breakable. God did not put his treasure in a crush-proof box, or a solid lead vault, or wrap it in styrofoam padding. He did not put his treasure with angels who never stub their toes or plastic saints you could drop from the Eiffel Tower without breaking them. Fragile earthen vessels he wanted. But this makes for pain and injury. You put clay pots next to each other, move them around, dust them off, let them get too close, and you will see damaged vessels – a cracked lip, a broken handle, a shattered vase. Mark this well, and take stock: if you agree to carry the treasure of God around, in the company of other earthen vessels, you are likely to become a cracked pot before you are finished (Smedes 1982:72).

Perceptive words. In the rough and tumble of life we often get hurt. Or we hurt others by our careless words and insensitive actions. The memories of past failures sting us. Will we stumble and fail again? Can God still use us, weak and bungling servants? Yes! He could have produced bionic men and women to carry out his purposes. He could have despatched Gabriel

169

and his angelic task-force to accomplish his will. But he chose us – fallible and fragile beings – so that he could display his power and glory through us. Vessels are meant to be filled. A cup is designed to be filled with water for drinking. A jar that is filled with oil provides light. As we are filled with God's Holy Spirit, we are able to function as his servants.

> Jesus, fill now with Thy Spirit
> Hearts that full surrender know;
> That the streams of living water
> From our inner man may flow.
>
> Channels only, blessed Master,
> But with all Thy wondrous power
> Flowing through us, Thou canst use us
> Ev'ry day and ev'ry hour.

> (From the hymn, 'How I praise Thee,
> Precious Saviour', by Mary E. Maxwell.)

Chapter Fourteen

WORKING WITH PROBLEM LEADERS

Wouldn't it be wonderful if we and everyone else on our leadership team always put Christ first? And if we were to serve and minister to God's people in a spirit of love, harmony and humility? Sadly, that's not the picture of many leadership teams. We are all tainted by sin, and even in our service we encounter tensions, problems and frustrations.

In chapter ten we glanced briefly at the famous 'one another' passages. God's Word bids us to accept, love, serve and care for one another. Sometimes tensions arise because of poor communication between leaders, particularly in the area of making decisions and implementing goals. We therefore offered some guidelines on corporate decision-making.

But no matter how much we try to apply God's Word and also to exercise sound management principles, we shall never be able totally to eradicate serious personality differences which cause problems. Leaders come from different backgrounds and possess different temperaments. Some think and act faster than others. They are like the accelerator in a car. Others by contrast are cautious and are sometimes accused of pressing on the brakes too frequently.

When we find it hard to get along with others, we may complain, 'How I wish I could work with another team of leaders! I didn't pick this bunch – I was simply appointed to serve on this committee.' But the Sovereign Lord often has a purpose. Learning to work with others is part of his process in sanctifying us. It's never easy and it's often painful. But God does give grace and special wisdom to cope with problem people.

Joe was the secretary of his Christian fellowship. He somehow sensed that Terry didn't see eye to eye with him on some key issues. Whenever he came up with a brilliant idea, Terry gave at least three reasons why the proposal would not work. Being the treasurer, Terry could use money – or rather the lack of it – as an excuse for not embarking on certain ventures. Joe could have just tried to ignore his fellow leader, but that would not have solved the problem because he still had another ten months to serve alongside him. Yes, he could have simply roughed it out – after all, ten months is not all that long. But deep in his heart, Joe felt that that would not be the lesson that God was wanting him to learn from this rather strained relationship.

One day when they were alone together in Joe's room, almost at the same time they both remarked that they had never got to know each other properly in an informal setting. They only had a working relationship, forged in the atmosphere of committee and business meetings. Joe broached the subject of their uneasy relationship. Terry thought for a few moments, then said, 'I am glad you have brought this up. As you know, I am more of an introvert. And probably because of my maths background, I tend to be rather cautious and calculating. You, on the other hand, keep coming up with new ideas and throwing them at us. So I see it as my duty to put forward the opposite point of view every time. . . . It's this idea of Hegel's: you propound a thesis, I express the antithesis and I hope that the rest of the committee will come out with the synthesis. But I have recently detected that more often than not there is an awkward silence.' And as they continued the conversation, Joe realized that he had unconsciously projected the image of an uncaring visionary. He had always been the ideas-and-action man. He was rather ashamed that he had not felt and prayed more for Terry who, he discovered, was struggling with several family problems. His parents' marriage was on the rocks and his older brother had been involved in a nasty road accident. They finally ended their time together in prayer, confessing their sins to the Lord, and when Terry left, they hugged one another, thankful that God had helped them to heal their rift.

But not all leaders are open to God. Do you remember Diotrephes? The apostle John had a hard time with this leader. Diotrephes loved to be first (3 John 9), and he was actively engaged in a gossip campaign against the apostle (verse 10). This arrogant fellow was also inhospitable and had expelled some believers from his local congregation. It seems that no-one could handle Diotrephes, but the apostle John clearly intimates that he would have to discipline him personally (verse 10). Thankfully, this is an extreme case. If we have to deal with the modern equivalents of Diotrephes – domineering leaders who are opposed to apostolic doctrine and practice – we too have to act with firmness. But we can only do this in partnership with others who are also convinced that the person needs disciplining. We must then confront him with firmness and love, and if he does not repent, decisive action must be taken to remove him from his position of spiritual leadership.

Other types of problem leaders

Problem leaders include those who cling to their privileged status but are not prepared to shoulder the responsibilities of leadership. Such leaders let the team down. Members suffer because these workers do not take their commitments seriously. They need to be reminded that leadership spells responsibility and they need motivating to do their job. Sometimes the reason why a person fails to perform duties is because he feels inadequately trained for a particular assignment. Although we love to see the faith of our fellow leaders stretched, it is important that we do not harm them by not giving them sufficient training, resources and backing.

Some of us face another chronic problem, that of leaders who are simply too busy. They have so many irons in the fire that they find it impossible to give their full attention to anything, and they fail to accomplish specific tasks. I once sat in a committee meeting where an extremely busy Christian leader began to address us on a couple of topics that were not on our agenda. He made some rather strange proposals and I noticed that everyone was beginning to feel uncomfortable and confused. After a while, the chairman asked him to clarify a particular proposal and he blurted out in horror, 'Oh, I'm so sorry! I was speaking about a project which was raised at the board meeting of . . .'!

Unfortunately, some organizations assume that they can only transact their business and fulfil their objectives if they have big names on their committees. I personally believe that it is important to have well-known Christian leaders to back our organizations but we do not have to suck them into our committees. Their names can simply appear on a special council of reference, giving the Christian public confidence in the work we do. Rather, we should always invite to be committee members people who are prepared to give priority to our fellowship or church, otherwise we will end up with excessively busy Christian leaders who are full of good intentions, but who will never be able to accomplish the task for which they have been appointed. It's always a wise policy to pick people who are prepared to work hard, even if they are not very experienced leaders.

Three is a useful number

A close friend of mine once said, 'There are always three sides to an argument: yours, mine and the truth!' She is right! One problem in our conversations with fellow leaders is that we do not always encode our message with precision and clarity which means that our hearers decode us wrongly. We can overcome this either by improving our communication and checking that the other person has decoded our message correctly, or better still, by the two of us agreeing to record in writing all decisions reached. But what if you have to work alongside someone with a different background who does not necessarily see eye to eye with you? Perhaps you have had strong personality clashes in the past. How can you work with this problem leader? I have found from experience that it is extremely helpful to have a third person present at your meetings and discussions. If we are strong leaders, we can be rather intransigent in our own opinions and find it very hard to appreciate the other person's point of view. A third person can help both parties to see things more objectively, thus defusing tensions and clearing up misunderstandings.

Even if I am on the best terms with another colleague, when it comes to crucial decisions I always find it useful to have a triumvirate. I am not claiming that we should be 'trinitarian' in our decision-making, but over and over again I have experienced the benefits of interaction between three people. If there are only two of us and we have opposite viewpoints, we will reach a stalemate. A trusted third person so often transforms the meeting, acts as a bridge between us and helps us to move forward together.

If you are finding it difficult to get on with another leader, you must first pray, asking God to search your own heart and attitudes (Psalm 139:23–24). Sometimes the problem is with us personally; we can have a jaundiced view of people. This is particularly true when we are tired or depressed. We need first to get right with God.

If, however, we have sought to identify the problem that is affecting our relationship with another leader and it seems that the fault lies with them, what should we do? We are not simply to dismiss it nor to bear a grudge against them. Instead we are to speak the truth in love (Ephesians 4:15). For some of us, this could involve making ourselves vulnerable, for in doing so we lay ourselves open to their criticisms and perhaps even rejection. But loving leadership always seeks to clear blocks in communication and relationships.

A cardinal principle in working with others, especially those who may differ from us and those whom we find it hard to get along with, is to stress our common allegiance to the Lord Jesus. He is our common Lord and he is the one who can bring us together. He specializes in breaking down barriers! He is the one who can help us to love one another and to serve together in his kingdom.

Chapter Fifteen

AFFIRMING LEADERS

Ask leaders what they cherish most from their fellow workers and church members. Their reply could probably be expressed in one word – affirmation.

Leaders carry heavy loads. They face crises. Some are handicapped by personal weaknesses. Others may be haunted by a sense of failure or may be smarting under criticism. A word of appreciation can make a beleaguered leader's day! I once saw a fellow leader burst into tears when an old lady came up to him and said, 'Don, I know you are going through a tough time. I am praying every day that God will give you strength.'

Once, when some of my close friends asked me what I had done during my last overseas trip, they were rather taken aback when I said, 'I stopped two people from resigning.' No, I wasn't the master problem-solver! In both cases, all I did was to listen to these two dear brothers. One was a pastor and the other a general secretary of an IFES movement. Both felt discouraged and misunderstood. The general secretary had been working for eight years, and no-one had ever told him whether he was doing a good job or not. They had taken him for granted. He had given all he had to student work and somehow there was no word of appreciation.

At a consultation with my senior co-workers, we discussed our rôle and our relationship to younger colleagues. Someone said, 'Sometimes we may need to be bishops confirming our younger brethren.' We were not using these terms in an ecclesiastical sense. We were reminding ourselves of our responsibility to affirm others.

Young leaders are often plagued by doubts. Are they in the

right job? Are they fulfilling their responsibilities adequately? Are their performances in keeping with the expectations of those who appointed them? What they desperately need is words of encouragement.

When we turn to the Scriptures, we can track down various occasions on which particular leaders received affirmation. Joshua is a classic case. He was appointed to succeed Moses, the outstanding leader and lawgiver. Moses had been the pioneer. Joshua was assigned the task of occupying Canaan and building up the nation of Israel. What a gigantic portfolio!

The Lord knew that Joshua required assurance and confirmation of his leadership. So God bolstered his servant's confidence with these reassuring and challenging words:

'As I was with Moses, so I will be with you; I will never leave you or forsake you.

'Be strong and courageous, because you will lead these people to inherit the land . . . Be strong and very courageous. Be careful to obey all the law my servant Moses gave you; do not turn from it to the right or to the left, that you may be successful wherever you go . . . Have I not commanded you? Be strong and courageous. Do not be terrified; do not be discouraged, for the LORD your God will be with you wherever you go' (Joshua 1:5–9).

In a private encounter with Peter, Jesus Christ warned his cocksure disciple that Satan was going to sift him like wheat. Our Lord predicted Peter's denial. But that was not going to be the end of the story. When the apostle was restored, he was to *strengthen* his brethren (Luke 22:31–32).

Those who have experienced dark moments in their spiritual pilgrimage, but have also received God's forgiving grace, must not selfishly go their own way. They have an added responsibility to strengthen their brothers and sisters. In Acts, we see Peter travelling extensively. His objective was to encourage and confirm the faith of young converts.

On his first missionary journey, Paul and his team had established churches in Lystra, Iconium and Antioch. They later revisited these churches, and Luke describes their activities in terms of 'strengthening the disciples and encouraging them to remain true to the faith' (Acts 14:22). The same word *episterizō* is used in Acts 15:41. There it describes Paul's mission in Syria and Cilicia – he was strengthening the churches. We must remember that these were young churches and most of their members were but fledglings. They had believed the gospel and been taught basic doctrine. Now the foundations of their faith had to be fortified. Thorough apostolic teaching would help them to build their superstructure.

I sometimes visit Christians who live and work in countries where they are a tiny minority. Some have come to faith in Christ amidst family opposition. As I seek to expound God's Word to them, I see their eyes sparkling and faces beaming. I can almost hear them thinking, 'Yes, this is what we have been reading. It confirms our beliefs.'

Tired pastors and missionaries also need to be confirmed by God's Word. Many can testify to blessings received at conferences where there are Bible readings. These expositions are a source of great refreshment. Perhaps they have been encountering demonic attacks and every step of faith has been challenged by the Evil One. Or they may be discouraged by the lack of response to the gospel. Bible teaching that points to the sufficiency of Christ and the resources of his Spirit reinforces faith and produces fresh commitment.

Means of affirmation

We have hinted at the importance of conferences. There is also immense value in face-to-face meetings. It might sound strange, but many young leaders receive astonishing encouragement from meeting stalwarts of the faith.

One of my co-workers, Samuel Escobar, told me about his first visit to Europe in 1959 to attend a major IFES gathering. Three years before, he had been invited by Dr John White, the IFES Associate General Secretary for Latin America, to serve as a student worker in Peru. Samuel's task was to establish an ongoing student witness in the campuses of his home country. During those three years he had been receiving books and magazines from other IFES movements. He found tremendous inspiration in the sermons of Dr Martyn Lloyd-Jones, and also the reports of the exploits of Inter-Varsity Fellowship, the British student movement. So when he arrived in Paris he was overjoyed, because Dr Lloyd-Jones was there as the President of IFES. Samuel said that just to shake the Doctor's hand was for him a mighty affirmation of his ministry as a student worker. Later he left Paris and went to Cambridge, the historic home of evangelical student witness, where he met up with other Christian leaders. All these experiences motivated Samuel to new heights of service.

Letters can be another means of affirming leaders. We have somehow lost the art of letter-writing. This is probably because of cheaper 'phone calls and dearer postage! But a generation ago, many outstanding Christian leaders were known for their letter-writing ministry. Contrary to popular belief, they did not write long treatises, but would pen brief notes, sometimes on postcards. I recall once receiving a hand-written note from the late Bishop Frank Houghton. We had met briefly at a missionary council meeting. He had learnt that I had become associate pastor of the Chinese church in London. Imagine my surprise and delight to receive a letter from this man of God! A few lines and a brief quotation from Scripture – that was all that Bishop Houghton had written, but that note was a source of tremendous encouragement to me.

In the IFES office we send birthday cards to our staff and their spouses. A simple touch, but one that means a great deal to them. As leaders, we should always be asking ourselves whether there is somebody we can encourage by a letter or telephone call.

Failure to affirm others

Why do we fail in the ministry of affirmation? We fail because we are too wrapped up in ourselves. We want others to appreciate us and we forget to empathize with others. Affirmation means much more than uttering clichés of praise or even the routine 'phone call. We affirm people by giving them time. If someone comes to us for a chat and we are busy shuffling papers around or our eyes roam over the room, they can become even more dispirited by the time they leave. To affirm is to listen attentively.

Some of us confuse affirmation with flattery. I once heard a pastor telling two octogenarian ladies in his congregation that they looked hardly a day older than thirty! That's flattery, not affirmation! When we flatter, we want to give the other person a psychological boost to make them feel good. Often what we say is only half true. We sometimes have ulterior motives when we flatter people.

But as leaders, we should be generous in expressing appreciation. For example, a member has spent long hours assembling an exhibition. Everyone has found it most illuminating. We should personally commend this member on his splendid efforts.

Affirmation does not mean the absence of criticism. When we see a younger leader or member sinning, we do them ill by not rebuking and correcting them. The Scriptures bid us speak the truth in love (Ephesians 4:15). Truth exposes sin; it points to God's light and standards. So our task as leaders is to help the erring Christian face up to the truth about himself and his sin. We do not assume the role of prosecutor, pointing an accusing finger at his faults. We shouldn't criticize someone in such a way as to make him feel small, insignificant and useless. We are to speak the truth *in love*. Love means wanting the best for a brother or sister. Therefore it grieves me to see them walking in darkness. I desire their well-being so I yearn for them to walk with God. Loving rebuke is in fact an expression of affirmation.

My wife King Ling has a remarkable gift for affirming Christians. Once a leader of a Bible study group was behaving obnoxiously towards his group members. He kept harping on about his own achievements and belittling the contributions of others. I am afraid that if I had had to counsel him, I would probably have used rather barbed words.

King Ling spent time with him. She lovingly confronted him with his faults. He knew that my wife was not out to get at him. They worked through the problem together, and later, after a time of prayer, he emerged ten feet tall! This brother had been rebuked and affirmed. Reproof, though at times

180

painful, is meant to heal rather than destroy. Like the surgeon's knife, rebuke, that is 'speaking the truth in love', removes diseased tissues, its over-all objective being to bring healing and wholeness.

Predecessors and successors

We deal now with a rather sensitive topic – the need of the Christian community to affirm both the successor and predecessor.

Jonathan was appointed the director of a fair-sized missionary organization. For six months before he assumed his responsibilities as the chief executive officer, his predecessor, Mark, showed him the ropes. Both men respected each other and worked harmoniously together during the period of orientation. Mark then retired to a seaside haven. During his first year, Jonathan travelled to various mission-fields. He got on well with all the missionaries and also with the office team. But at the beginning of his second year, a dark cloud descended upon him. Hardly a week passed without 'phone calls and notes from his predecessor.

Each time Mark assured Jonathan that it was out of concern that he was communicating with him. He said that some of the prayer-partners had expressed dissatisfaction with the new policies of the mission and were even questioning Jonathan's judgment. Mark pestered Jonathan relentlessly, and got all his friends to rally to his support. Before long, the matter was brought before the board.

Fortunately the board chairman acted decisively. First he assured Jonathan of his unstinting support. With Jonathan's permission, he and another senior member of the committee went to meet Mark. They listened patiently to his concerns and complaints. At the same time they firmly but graciously told him that Jonathan must be given a free rein to exercise his leadership.

All credit to the chairman for protecting Jonathan. He was wise in taking a senior member of the board with him to meet Mark. The latter recognized that he had overstepped the mark in interfering in the affairs of the mission.

The loyal support of the chairman did Jonathan the world of good. Without that affirmation he would have had great difficulty in operating as the leader of the mission.

The chairman also understood Mark's predicament. He sensed that it wasn't easy for a man who had given the best years of his life to the mission to keep his fingers out of the administrative pie. Retirement hadn't turned out to be a pleasant experience. Mark, like many Christian leaders, had found his value in his work. Moreover, he had been ably supported by the office team. His secretary used to type all his letters, but in his retirement he had to write everything by hand. He also missed the hustle and bustle of office life and the excitement of travelling and ministering in different countries.

Churches, missionary societies and Christian organizations should assist their senior workers in this period of transition. Once I asked a missionary whether he was looking forward to his retirement. He shook his head and lamented, 'To be honest, I feel as if I am going to be dumped on the rubbish heap.'

This faithful band of warriors who have given so much of their lives to God's service need to be affirmed. A public farewell is often appropriate. Besides making financial arrangements such as pension benefits, churches and societies should encourage these leaders to get involved in their local churches. Wholehearted involvement in a local church might take the boredom out of retirement. These servants of Christ should also be encouraged to intercede diligently for others. Faithful intercessors have a vital role to play in God's kingdom enterprise. The older people get, the greater their desire to feel wanted.

Whatever our position in the church or Christian fellowship, we all have a ministry of encouragement. Why not seek out a leader and assure him of your prayers and support? What about voicing appreciation to someone for sticking so faithfully to a routine job? A word of praise for those who have put long hours into running a conference or special event would make their day. Who knows? Your words may encourage them to attempt greater things for God! We can't show appreciation by keeping our mouths shut!

The ministry of affirmation is beautifully illustrated in the third Servant Song:

> The Sovereign LORD has given
> > me an instructed tongue,
> > to know the word that
> > sustains the weary.
> He wakens me morning by
> > morning,
> > wakens my ear to listen like
> > one being taught (Isaiah 50:4).

Spiritual leaders, like the Servant, are trainee teachers. We are pupils in God's school. As we listen daily to him through his Word, he confirms and strengthens us. We in turn can sustain the weary. God will give us fitting words to affirm them so they too will be strengthened and cheered in their service for the Lord.

Chapter Sixteen

GOOD ENDINGS

Wang Ming-Dao, the fearless preacher of Beijing, China, once wrote: 'Many have good beginnings, but few have good endings' (quoted by Adeney 1985:77). These words were penned by a leader who had suffered much for his faith both under the Japanese and the Marxists. By his life and words he urged a generation of Chinese Christians to stand firm in the Lord.

Good beginnings? Many Christians make promising starts. They respond enthusiastically to their leadership assignments. When the weather's fair and the going's good, they advance steadily. But when the storms break, they are overwhelmed and retire to the sidelines.

The road of leadership is never smooth. We shall encounter opposition and obstacles in every shape and form. The devil will hurl the fiery darts of doubt. He will seek to seduce us and direct us away from God's path. We may face criticisms and discouragement. Like God's servants in the Bible we will not be immune from stress, depression, persecution and self-doubt. Sometimes we are handicapped by poor health. As we search the Scriptures, we observe that leadership was never plain sailing for Abraham, Moses, Joshua, David, Elijah, Amos, Isaiah, Jeremiah, Ezekiel, Daniel, Ezra, Nehemiah, Paul, Peter, Stephen and a host of others. But God kept them going despite setbacks and repeated failures.

It has been said, 'When the going gets tough, the tough get going.' Our toughness is not necessarily an in-built quality, neither is it a stoic grin-and-bear-it attitude to pain and suffering. God toughens us as we rely on his grace and power.

Good ending: the example of Caleb

One of my favourite Old Testament characters is Caleb. I've always been inspired by the qualities of this remarkable leader. At eighty-five years old, well past retirement age, he was still fighting fit. Listen to these fantastic words from the lips of this veteran leader:

> 'I am still as strong today as the day Moses sent me out; I'm just as vigorous to go out to battle now as I was then' (Joshua 14:11).

Then he made this amazing request to Joshua: 'Give me this mountain' (verse 12, AV/KJV).

Caleb was not content to rest on his laurels or to look back on his golden past. Indeed, he had a remarkable track record as a warrior and leader. But with God's help he wanted to go on fighting and staking new claims for his tribe and people.

What are the secrets of this great man of God?

Caleb followed the Lord wholeheartedly (verse 8)

His commitment to the Lord was total. Once he had set his heart to follow God, there was no turning back. Retreat was never in his vocabulary. His supreme ambition was to do the will of the Sovereign Commander.

At the age of forty, he was one of the twelve intelligence officers sent by Moses to spy out the land. All twelve men were impressed by what they saw. The land of Canaan was very fertile and fruitful and had tremendous potential. But according to the majority report, a military invasion was out of the question. The fortified cities were peopled by giants! The Israelites were grasshoppers by comparison (Numbers 13:33)! However, Caleb and Joshua disassociated themselves from this pessimistic view. Rather, they affirmed, 'We should go up and take possession of the land, for we can certainly do it' (verse 30). Both men were warriors of faith; they knew who their supreme Commander was. They were not afraid to nail their colours to the mast. With God, they would triumph.

Their words had hardly left their mouths when they were

met with the chilly and cynical stares of the other ten spies. 'Stop acting as wise guys. The Canaanites are too powerful – we are no match for them!' But Caleb and Joshua would not give in. They urged Moses and the entire assembly to wage a campaign against the Canaanites. Sadly the majority report prevailed.

God then gave his verdict. The ten spies and all the adult members of Israel would perish in the wilderness because of their unbelief. The Lord specially commended Caleb, stating, 'My servant Caleb has a different spirit and follows me *wholeheartedly*' (Numbers 14:24).

God expects total, not partial, commitment today. If we hold back, we shall not win the battle of faith. But if we serve him wholeheartedly, he honours our stand and will do mighty things through us.

Caleb had a different perspective (Numbers 14:24)

This is another of Caleb's secrets which made him such an outstanding leader.

The ten spies gave a one-sided report. Their evaluation was based on the fact that from a human point of view, the situation seemed impossible. How could a rabble band of liberated slaves with limited resources and military experience defeat the superior forces of the Canaanites? From a human viewpoint their assessment was correct. But unlike Caleb, they left the Mighty Lord out of their reckoning. Israel was his covenant people and he had entered into a special contract with them (see Exodus 19:5f.). Had he not overthrown the armies of Egypt? Had he not guided his people with his own presence? So what were fortified cities or giant soldiers? Caleb knew his God and therefore had the courage to ask, 'Why not?'

In 1966 I made my first visit to Thailand. Several missionary magazines were vividly reminding readers that there were more Buddhist temples in Thailand than individual Christians. I flew to Bangkok to explore the possibility of establishing an ongoing student witness in the campuses of this Buddhist country. Soon after my arrival, a veteran missionary took me aside and commented wryly, 'Our Presbyterian church has been here for just over a hundred years and we are still a tiny minority. The church is weak and struggling. Frankly, I think you have come to the wrong place to start student work. I would urge you to concentrate on your fine work in Singapore, Malaysia, the Philippines and Hong Kong. Don't waste your time in Thailand.'

I prayed in silence that God would prove him wrong! I am so glad that God answered that prayer! I found two Christian lecturers in two universities who were seeking to study the Bible with Thai students. So I encouraged them both to persevere. Three years later, one of the lecturers had to return to his home country, but he left behind him a Bible study group of four Christian students. He invited a young missionary to train these students and to spawn groups in other universities.

In 1970, my colleague Ada Lum and I were invited to a training conference attended by eight Thai students together with the young missionary. I had the responsibility of teaching the students how to share their faith with others. Half way through our week of training I suggested that they should have some practical field-work in the village market near our campsite. The Thai students protested, saying, 'We Thais are very polite. We can't just go and talk to strangers about Jesus Christ.' I replied, 'We Chinese are also very polite, but it's not a matter of courtesy! It's a matter of our willingness to obey Christ's command to be his witnesses.' So after some friendly persuasion they agreed to go and witness in twos. For a couple of hours they shared the good news of Jesus with shopkeepers, fishmongers and butchers, and discovered the joy of articulating their faith.

Later, as they returned in our Volkswagen minibus, the students were leaping and praising God! We got back to the camp and one of the students excitedly declared, 'A fishmonger that I spoke to told me that it was the first time that he had heard about the Lord Jesus from the lips of one of his own countrymen. He told me that a few years ago some foreigners with blond hair and long noses, speaking unintelligible Thai, had tried to tell him about a foreign god called Jesus. He said that today he had actually been able to understand.'

Soon after the training conference I had to leave to visit our movement in Vietnam, but my co-worker Ada Lum remained in Bangkok for six months. Her primary task was to encourage the students to have Bible studies and to invite their non-Christian friends along to examine the claims of Christ. During this period these eight Thai students witnessed a remarkable turning of students to Jesus Christ. In less than two years, every campus had an active Christian fellowship. The student leaders themselves met for prayers at 5.30 in the morning. They laid hold of God and he did mighty things in their midst. These Thai Christian students possessed a different attitude. They did not succumb to their image as an insignificant minority. Faith in God leads his people to do great exploits for him. It is this perspective that carries us forward.

Christian leaders often succumb to the spirit of the age. We become cynical when the Word of God appears to fall on barren ground. We spend endless hours analysing and discussing impossible situations and some people even write PhD's on them! Sometimes our Christian fellowships or churches get stuck in a rut and we fail to ask what difference it would make if we brought God into the situation. Faith dares to ask for the impossible. Think of Caleb and Joshua surveying the superior forces of the Canaanites; one look at God made them ask, 'Why not?'!

This is the spirit that makes great leaders. Think of William Carey in the eighteenth century. When he shared his concern to serve God as a missionary in India, the leaders of the Baptist denomination threw cold water on his plans. In their pious theological jargon, they told this cobbler from Northampton that God would evangelize the heathen in India. But William Carey had a totally different spirit. He followed God *wholeheartedly*, and one of the stirring slogans of this missionary pioneer finds an echo in many hearts today: Attempt great things for God, expect great things from God!'

Like the walls of Jericho, situations may look insurmountable, but let's never forget that our God is the great wall-breaker! By his Spirit, he initiates breakthroughs. He acts in ways beyond our wildest dreams and expectations. But we need to have the vision and courage to ask, 'Why not?'. Can God not do great things for people?

Caleb was never an irresponsible visionary. He was always conscious that God was spurring his people on to claim new ground. His view was God-centred. After all, it was God who was leading his people forward and he would give the land to them (Numbers 14:8). Therefore the people should not rebel against God, nor should they be afraid of the inhabitants of the land. Why not? Because ' "the LORD is with us" ' (verse 9). Caleb possessed a different spirit – that of complete confidence in the living God.

Don't we need that same spirit today? Consider the task of world evangelism. There are vast areas in our world where the church is weak and the masses have yet to hear about God's love as shown in Christ Jesus. He has given us his marching orders to 'go and make disciples of all nations' (Matthew 28:19). Aren't we tempted to say, 'Impossible. The Muslims, the Hindus and the Western secularists are resistant and even hostile to the Christian message'? World evangelism and disciple-making are uphill tasks. They are fraught with difficulties and dangers. But the risen Christ has also promised, 'I will be with you always, to the very end of the age' (verse 20). Surely that should infuse fresh heart into our endeavours for him.

Caleb always pressed forward

At the ripe old age of eighty-five, this remarkable leader did not speak of retirement plans. He took on fresh challenges: ' "Now give me this mountain" ' (Joshua 14:12, RSV). He wasn't content simply to live in the plains of everyday life. He could have sat by his fire-side talking to his grandchildren about the mighty exploits of the past. What fabulous tales they would have heard! But Caleb would not live in the glories of the past. He wanted to keep on fighting.

Here we have the third secret of a godly leader. We need to keep on fighting and pressing forward. Caleb wanted to die with his boots on. He thrived on fresh challenges. Every new step of faith leads us to the source of power – the Lord himself.

I am always touched when I speak to men and women of God who are still serving him in their seventies and eighties. Their physical vigour may be impaired, but their vision to serve

God has never diminished. They may not be positioned in the front line, but this noble company of prayer warriors knows what it means to seek the face of God to back up the troops. Sometimes, through their physical infirmities, we catch a glimpse of their exuberant spirit. They enjoy their Lord's company; they look forward to the day when they will see him face to face.

To have a good ending, we need to be fighting fit spiritually. In the battle there will be no time for idleness and complaints. We shall make it our constant aim to please him and to know him (see 2 Corinthians 5:9; Philippians 3:10). We will echo the objective of the apostle Paul: 'I consider my life worth nothing to me, if only I may finish the race and complete the task the Lord Jesus has given me – the task of testifying to the gospel of God's grace' (Acts 20:24). In our more sober moments, we may wonder how we are going to achieve this, and like Paul, we cry out, 'Who is equal to such a task?' (2 Corinthians 2:16). How can we possibly fulfil our God-given responsibilities as leaders? But with Paul, we look to God and declare with his same confidence, 'Our competence comes from God' (2 Corinthians 3:5). He is able!

BIBLIOGRAPHY

Adeney, D.H., *China: The Church's Long March* (Ventura: Regal Books (Gospel Light), 1985).

Alexander, J.W., *Managing Our Work* (Downers Grove: InterVarsity Press, 1975).

Barclay, O.R., *Whatever Happened to the Jesus Lane Lot?* (Leicester: Inter-Varsity Press, 1977).

Barclay, *Developing a Christian Mind* (Leicester: Inter-Varsity Press, Grand Rapids: Zondervan, 1983).

Barrett, C.K., *The First Epistle to the Corinthians* (New York: Harper & Row, 1968).

Barrs, J., *Freedom and Discipleship* (Leicester: Inter-Varsity Press, 1983).

Bonar, A.A., *Memoirs and Remains of the Reverend R. Murray M'Cheyne* (London: Oliphants, 1892).

Bridge, D. and Phypers, D., *Spiritual Gifts and the Church* (London: Inter-Varsity Press, 1973).

Coleman, R.E., *The Master Plan of Evangelism* (New Jersey: Revell, 1963).

Copley, D., *Taking a Lead* (Eastbourne: Kingsway, 1985).

Cranfield, C.E.B., *Romans* (ICC series), Vol. 2 (Edinburgh: T. & T. Clark, 1983).

Eddison, J., *Bash* (Basingstoke: Marshalls, 1983).

Engstrom, T.W., *The Making of a Christian Leader* (Grand Rapids: Zondervan, 1976).

Foulkes, F., *Ephesians* (Tyndale Commentaries) (London: Inter-Varsity Press, Grand Rapids: Eerdmans, 1963).

Gibbs, E., *I Believe in Church Growth* (rev. ed.) (London: Hodder & Stoughton, 1985).

Green, M., *I Believe in the Holy Spirit* (London: Hodder & Stoughton, 1974).

Greenslade, P., *Leadership* (Basingstoke: Marshalls, 1984).

Griffiths, M., *Shaking the Sleeping Beauty* (Leicester: Inter-Varsity Press, 1980).

Guthrie, D., *The Pastoral Epistles* (Tyndale Commentaries) (London: Inter-Varsity Press, Grand Rapids: Eerdmans, 1957).

191

Le Peau, A.T., *Paths of Leadership* (Downers Grove: InterVarsity Press, 1983).

Lloyd-Jones, D.M., *Authority* (London: Inter-Varsity Press, 1958).

Lum, A. ,and Siemens, R., *Creative Bible Studies* (Bombay: Gospel Literature Service, 1973).

MacDonald, G., *Ordering Your Private World* (Nashville: Nelson, 1984, Crowborough: Highland Books, 1986).

Mallone, G., *Those Controversial Gifts* (Downers Grove: InterVarsity Press, 1983).

Mallone, *Furnace of Renewal* (Downers Grove: InterVarsity Press, 1981).

Milne, B., *We Belong Together* (Leicester: Inter-Varsity Press, 1978).

Morris, L., *The Gospel According to St. John* (London: Marshall, Morgan & Scott, 1972).

Moule, H.C.G., *To My Younger Brethren* (London: Hodder & Stoughton, 1892).

Ortiz, J.C., *Disciple* (Basingstoke: Lakeland, 1976).

Prior, D., *The Church in the Home* (Basingstoke: Marshall, 1983).

Prior, *The Message of 1 Corinthians* (BST series) (Leicester and Downers Grove: Inter-Varsity Press, 1985).

Sanders, J.O., *Spiritual Leadership* (London: Marshall, Morgan & Scott, 1967).

Sanders, *Paul the Leader* (Eastbourne: Kingsway, 1983).

Smedes, L.B., *How Can It Be All Right When Everything Is All Wrong?* (New York: Harper & Row, 1982).

Snyder, H.A., *The Problem of Wineskins* (Downers Grove: Inter-Varsity Press, 1975).

Snyder, *The Community of the King* (Downers Grove: InterVarsity Press, 1977).

Snyder, *The Radical Wesley* (Downers Grove: InterVarsity Press, 1980).

Snyder, *Liberating the Church* (Downers Grove: InterVarsity Press, 1983).

Stott, J.R.W., *The Preacher's Portrait* (London: Tyndale Press, 1961).

Stott, *Baptism and Fullness* (Leicester: Inter-Varsity Press, 1975).

Stott, *God's New Society* (The Message of Ephesians – BST series) (Leicester and Downers Grove: Inter-Varsity Press, 1979).

Stott, *I Believe in Preaching* (London: Hodder & Stoughton, 1982).

Stott, *Issues Facing Christians Today* (Basingstoke: Marshalls, 1984).

Taylor, J.V., *The Go-Between God* (London: SCM Press, 1972).

Tidball, D., *Skilful Shepherds* (Leicester: Inter-Varsity Press, Grand Rapids: Zondervan, 1986).

White, J., *Excellence in Leadership: the pattern of Nehemiah* (Downers Grove, Leicester: Inter-Varsity Press, 1986).

White, J. and Blue, K., *Healing the Wounded* (Downers Grove, Leicester: Inter-Varsity Press, 1985).